ENCOUNTERING CHRIST

Lay Witness...One Key to Renewal

BY

ROBERT L. MAIN

1908 Grand Avenue, Nashville, Tennessee 37203

Library of Congress Catalog Card Number: 72-129550

G032B: 670

ACKNOWLEDGMENT

The book is dedicated to all the witnesses, coordinators, pastors, and members of host churches who made the study possible; to my wife Marian who is a constant source of encouragement and a splendid witness; and to Charlotte Boswell who has done all the clerical and typing work on the study and manuscript.

CONTENTS

INTRODUCTION

Where to begin? Where to end? A study such as this has to have a beginning place. And it must have an ending, or at least a set of boundaries. So we've established some boundaries. This study will involve churches in Oklahoma, Texas, New Mexico and one in Arizona. This will peg it to the Southwest.

To further limit the scope we decided to use only churches where witnesses or participants from Christ United Methodist Church had attended missions. In addition we chose only witnesses from the teams serving those churches, and further limited it to people living in the four southwestern states.

This necessitated sacrificing the help and guidance and personal witness of many persons from other states who have helped in these four states. But again we felt the need to narrow the scope of our efforts. To those left out we say, "We love you and please forgive us."

"Many miracles and wonders were done through the apostles which caused everyone to be filled with awe." (Acts 2:43)

1

Renewal in Albuquerque

"Pastor, do you want to be a new preacher with a new church?" These words greeted me as I answered the phone one Sunday afternoon in the late spring of 1968. On the other end of the line was the young chairman of the evangelism commission of Christ United Methodist Church of Albuquerque, New Mexico.

Suspecting what he meant, and certainly not wanting to put a damper on his enthusiasm, I managed to answer that indeed I did want to be a new preacher with a new church. There followed from him a happy outpouring of spirit-filled excitement as he related to me what had happened to him and what he had seen happen to a lot of other people.

He had just come from a lay witness mission at Paradise Hills United Methodist, a small fairly new church on the mesa west of town. At my urging this highly rated technician at a major atomic energy installation and a part-time engineering student at the University of New Mexico had gone at the close of exams on Friday afternoon to look in on the mission. Tired and clobbered with responsibilities, he had gone out of loyalty to his pastor. He found so many exciting, contagious things going on that he couldn't stay away and returned for each event on the calendar.

The lay witness program came to New Mexico from two separate channels which became entwined one with the other. In the East a Ph.D. in bio-chemistry had given up a career in that field and had entered the ministry. Wanting to migrate to New Mexico he had accepted the pastorate of Paradise Hills

Church there. Having crossed paths with the witness movement in New England and having heard Tap Hanson at a retreat he was anxious to try a mission at his new church.

About the same time the veteran pastor at First Church, Roswell, New Mexico, some leaders in the field of evangelism, and I attended the annual meeting of the Council on Evangelism in San Antonio, Texas. There we were thrilled to hear Ben Johnson, Tap Hanson, and Tank Harrison, household names in the lay witness mission movement.

We had read Ben's writings and so heard him with great pleasure. Tap, the perfect southern gentleman, won the quick respect of the council. Tank rolled us in the aisles with his story of how he resisted the program until the Spirit caught up with him.

The New Mexico delegation came away excited with the possibilities. Our retiring conference board of evangelism immediately programmed a pilot mission for Roswell's First United Methodist Church to which we would invite a minister and laymen from other churches in the conference. This program became one of the main thrusts of the conference board.

As the district director of evangelism and a member of the conference board I was in a position to encourage the pastor of Paradise Hills Church to proceed with his dream of a mission there, even if it would precede the pilot mission at Roswell.

When the chairman of evangelism at Christ Church returned from the Paradise Hills mission in May the membership and evangelism commission met that same night and approved a mission for the church. The official board passed a resolution of approval early in June.

Then began the task of informing our congregation and selling them on the desirability of a mission. Appeals were made to various groups, manuals were bought and handed out for reading. Backyard lawn meetings brought more people into the discussion.

Late in June Christ Church held a spiritual life retreat at Arrowhead Methodist Camp near Santa Fe. Special guests included the pastor's family and several couples from the Paradise Hills Church. A two hour period was set aside on Saturday afternoon to hear from these guests. It turned out to be a thrilling and contagious afternoon. The winsome witnesses captivated their hosts. This retreat was the clincher needed. In two weeks a lay witness mission chairman was chosen and twelve committee chairmen plus co-chairmen were recruited and a firm date for a mission requested.

Committee heads began to meet weekly for an hour of conversational prayer followed by a planning session. A quick rapport was established between the leaders and excitement began to mount during the summer months. We were determined to be fully organized and mentally and spiritually prepared.

The original prayer group, as individuals, began forming other prayer groups to pray for the mission. A twenty-four hour prayer vigil was scheduled and became a highlight for many.

Meanwhile I was doing my homework. The suggested books were bought, plus others in the field of renewal and small groups. These were eagerly read and six special sermons were prepared and delivered in advance of the mission. Included were "The Renewal of the Church," "The Ministry of the Laity," "The Power of the Personal Witness," and "The Renewing Work of the Holy Spirit."

In September some of our church members flew to a mission at the New Haven United Methodist Church in Tulsa. The spirit of joy they brought back added to the flame steadily growing among our faithful leaders.

Then I, now conference secretary of evangelism, went to help with the Roswell pilot mission. Six others went along to observe. There we caught the power of the Spirit through fellowship with Tap Hanson and Walter Albritton and the fine witnesses and the lovely host groups.

The Roswell mission did much for the local church and helped to spread the story of lay missions across the conference. Many excellent witnesses from Roswell have shared in other missions.

The seven Christ Church delegates to Roswell brought back just the added touch of eager witnessing to build Christ Church to a beautiful crescendo leading into our mission. As they say in basketball parlance "we were up for the game."

When the coordinator arrived he said, "Why, you've already had your renewal just getting ready." And when it was all over he declared it to be one of the best prepared missions in which he had participated. We stress the need to plow the ground thoroughly so the seed will have a proper place to grow.

Our mission had thirty adults and nine youth coming from five states. It was a finely balanced team, expertly put together by the coordinator. From the first team session to the close of the mission a sense of expectation was in the air. A packed fellowship hall greeted the witnesses. Twenty-six discussion groups filled all the nooks and crannies. The sharing hour that night made it evident that something was afoot.

The next morning reports from seventeen coffee groups indicated that nothing had been lost during the night. People had done some hard thinking and were ready to open up and to share. Most of the groups had trouble breaking up for the men's and women's luncheons at noon Saturday. The leaven of the Spirit was working during each luncheon. There is something present in a man-to-man luncheon or a woman-to-woman luncheon that can be found in no other way. A poem about a father's responsibility to his son struck a responsive chord with the men as they met at a barbecue place. The women had a chance for a one-to-one confrontation as they listened intently to each other's problems.

Our coordinator follows the practice of holding a session on Saturday afternoon to help us chart our spiritual growth. In our case it was the catalyst that broke the Holy Spirit loose in a great and marvelous way. Quiet tears of joy were abundant on all sides. Witnessing began to take on meaning. The honest confessions brought us to new heights.

A semi-active plumbing contractor who got in on the mission quite by accident said later, "I did not know how hungry I was until I came to the mission." And his wife reported that he paced the floor in his anxiety to get back to the supper hour program. His anticipation was shared by us all. He is now hard at work in the church.

The supper witnessing hour helped to set the stage for the very significant and meaningful discussions and prayer groups that followed. Some lasted until a quarter of twelve. Scores visited the altar of the church for periods of renewal and commitment. Assurances of a new life in Christ came to many that night.

The seven-thirty team session next morning found the witnesses a bit subdued from a lack of sleep but as they shared the results of the small groups of the night before spirits revived. They were ready to see the mission come to a great spiritual conclusion.

The eight-thirty service was well attended, the witnesses superb, and the altar time a time of great victory. The youth and adult classes that followed were further opportunities for witnessing and sharing. Church school people who had missed the mission were greatly surprised to find such a joyful spirit when they got to class.

The second service had even greater results. The whole front of the church was full of kneeling individuals committing and recommitting their lives to Christ and his church. When we arose from the altar a row of people was standing in front of me wanting, without prompting, to join our church. What a fitting climax to the morning services!

Then how grateful we were that we had planned a noon luncheon at the church. This gave us a chance for individual good-byes to each witness. The immense friendship circle and the many songs we sang seemed to band us into a permanent unbroken circle.

We then followed our coordinator's advice to put our feet up for an hour. It was our first rest pause since Friday. Our sighs were contented ones.

Then we began to wonder about the approaching six o'clock session. Would anybody come? Would anyone say anything? Would it be an anti-climax? These were needless anxieties.

We gathered informally in the sanctuary and sang "It Is

No Secret" and "How Great Thou Art." The pastor picked up a couple of wrinkled facial tissues, left over from the altar time of the morning, held them up and said, "I believe we have here the badge and symbol of the mission."

After a choked up statement of what the mission had meant to me, I turned the meeting over to our hard-working chairman. He wanted to know if anyone had anything to say—and the parade began. One after another adult and youth alike came forward. They asked a mate or a son or daughter to pray for them. Then with a radiant glow on their faces, the witnesses shared openly and honestly what had happened to them.

Occasionally someone came forward a second time, unable to restrain himself from a second chance to share. One leader made an impact when he said that he wanted to confess that he had harbored ill thoughts toward his pastor and the pastor's wife and he wanted to beg their forgiveness. This led to some tender moments.

En route home the coordinator called back and found us still going strong.

After three hours and twenty minutes of sharing we took an offering and officially closed the meeting. But a large group went to a nearby doughnut shop to continue sharing.

Here are excerpts from reactions of some of the persons attending the mission:

"Saturday night in the small groups I knew that I had to do something on my own. I knelt at the altar and prayed that the Lord might give me a sign. I prayed 'Lord, I need you, my family needs you.' And I knew then that I could do anything for the Lord."

"When the altar call was made and I went down there my heart was pounding and I thought this is like Christmas. And then I thought, 'It is Christmas, for Christmas represents the birth of Christ and this represents the rebirth of myself.' "

"At the team sessions when we paired off and were asked to project love to each other without saying anything I really knew then what this was all about."

"During the mission I realized that everything I had been doing, I had been doing for the wrong reasons."

"This is the most exciting thing that has happened to me. At the beginning of preparations for the mission I was on the fringe of things, maybe even a little resentful about the whole thing. I didn't want anything to happen in my life. I liked it just the way it was. When I found out we were going to have a witness couple stay with us it did not change things much. I still figured I could get out of attending all the sessions. But after I started the mission things began to happen. And I feel better every minute."

"This mission has been one of the greatest mountaintop experiences for me. I ask that you pray for me and my needs as a minister's wife."

"Thank you for the lay witness mission and for what it has done for me. I had asked the Lord to send me where he wanted to and I believe that he sent me to Albuquerque. Prayer is now the most important thing in my life."

"We were skeptical about the mission. We thought we would come Friday night and see what it was all about. And things began to happen. We listened to Jim as he said, 'I found Christ and I want to share.' We knelt with him in fellowship hall and knew that he had found Christ. All of us went to the altar when the call was made for we found that we had what Jim had."

"It is only in the past few years that I have been so critical of the church. It seemed that everyone was always so busy. But I kept coming, out of habit I guess. Now, I have found something and I ask that you keep me in your prayers so that I will keep what I have found."

"Through this mission Christ has become a reality to me and to my folks. There is one thing that can unite the young people and the older generation—Christ. I hope that I can keep him foremost in my life. You people in this church are really one body in Christ."

"I came seeking a cure-all. Maybe I didn't find that, but I found something. I'm issuing an invitation to anyone that wants to come to join us in a prayer group Tuesday night. Let's keep what we have found."

"Since coming to Christ Church I have prayed that as in

Acts we could all be of one accord. Praise God, this weekend I have seen it."

"Everything that I have done for Christ Church I have done in love because I love this church. But in all my doing I have said, 'Jesus, you can't keep up with me.' Right now I have never felt so humble. And from now on instead of running ahead of Jesus, I want to run with him."

"This mission has really made me see myself. I need your prayers for I'm going to try."

"The love that has been evidenced during this mission is tremendous. The hope of the church is in its laymen for they can bring the church back to the top."

"Tonight my cup really runneth over. I knew that this church had many wonderful Christians in it with much love for each other but that they just did not know it. I knew that if we could have a lay witness mission this love would come out. And it has. Everyone can truly say that we have a new church. But my greatest joy is that I can stand here and tell you that I have a new husband and I praise God for it."

WHO WERE INVOLVED?

What sort of people were caught up in the mission at Christ United Methodist Church? If you mean age—they ranged from twelve to eighty-one. If you mean vocations, they were schoolteachers, students, housewives, technicians, insurance salesmen, secretaries, buyers, engineers, noncommissioned and commissioned officers of Army and Air Force, nurses, doctors, and so on.

If you mean their place of leadership in the church—the official board chairman, the vice chairman of the board, the lay leader, the president of the WSCS, chairmen of WSCS circles, chairmen of membership and evangelism, missions, education, social concerns, worship and finance commissions, Sunday school teachers of all age groups, and trustees.

If you mean staff—choir director, organist, kindergarten teachers, business manager, and pastor.

Whereas this broad and deep influence on the leaders of the church may not occur in every church hosting a mission it certainly worked out that way in this church. Our people are now active in sub-district, district, and conference work through the WSCS, the way work, and through conference boards and committees.

WHAT ABOUT LATER?

1. *Prayer and sharing groups.* Almost without any apparent leadership twelve groups came into being to join the only permanent one we had had. They meet at night, after school, at 6:15 A.M. Saturday morning, or any time they can find open. The first ones after the mission were wonderful to behold. They were like a bunch of mini-pentecosts. Everyone had been reading some modern version of the Bible and wanted to share some discoveries. Five months later these groups still exist.

2. *Prayer at meetings.* Most all our meetings, official board and otherwise, are started with periods of conversational prayer. Our finance drive came on the heels of our mission and the imported leader was awed at the prayers he heard from our people.

3. *Other missions.* Reacting in the pattern followed by other missions our people have looked forward to sharing this with others. They have been on missions to Tulsa, Oklahoma; Roswell, New Mexico; Yuma, Arizona; Palo Alto, California; Baird, Texas; Spearman, Texas; El Paso, Texas; Alva, Oklahoma; Abilene, Texas; Gruver, Texas; Dalhart, Texas; Pecos, Texas; Dallas, Texas and have invitations to other missions set for the spring and summer. Several have become coordinators.

These returning witnesses add a new dimension to the prayer meetings and board meetings with their reports. The sharing of evaluations from other churches and letters received also add much to the sense of joy to be found in our prayer and share groups.

4. *Reading.* Our business manager has lost count of the copies of *Good News for Modern Man* and other books we've bought, sold, and read. Tank Harrison's booklet *I've Been Had* sells like the proverbial hotcakes.

5. *Study.* In addition to the books they read for home study,

people are also open to other opportunities for study. The mission study on the Gospel of John was used with great profit. A study of the Sermon on the Mount was eagerly anticipated.

6. *Local activity of witnesses.* Our witnesses show much interest in social concerns, in missions, and in evangelism. Calling is done at least three times a week and the witnesses carry more than their share. They also carry their choir and teaching chores as before. Our church sponsors and staffs a day kindergarten in a depressed neighborhood. Many of our people are involved with the school.

7. *Closer relationship of pastor and people.* People are praying more for their pastor than before. When they come individually and in small groups, without prompting, to pray for the pastor just before the service, a sense of warmth and support pervades the entire service. A pastor cannot help but be lifted by these experiences of supportive prayer.

8. *Other witnessing.* The pastor and laymen of the church have had many chances to witness to others of their newfound joy. District conferences, Women's Societies, district men's retreats, as well as conference program councils have heard our witnesses. Prayer groups, commission members, official boards, and other congregations have called on our men and women to witness as a part of a plan to encourage a mission in their church.

9. *Tape-O-Grams.* As a means of keeping our small groups alive and fresh we subscribe to and use the tapes prepared by the Institute for Church Renewal. These are adding much to the deepening of our own spiritual insights and to the strengthening of our own resolves and commitments. On the reverse side of the tapes are wise suggestions for leaders of small groups.

10. *No claim to perfection.* None of the people at this church would claim to have arrived. We are quick to agree that we've taken only a preliminary step or two on a long journey into faith; but they are steps taken with confidence that we're pointed in the right direction.

ONE MAN'S PERSPECTIVE

To get a proper balance perhaps you would like to read the comments of our membership chairman as he wrote from the stance of five months later.

"The preparation for our lay witness mission was a period of anticipation. The prayer groups formed prior to the mission were the first real fellowship groups that I had been a part of. The committees and mechanics needed to put on a mission helped people come to know each other much better.

"The Sunday evening evaluation session was very meaningful. It was heart warming to hear people be honest and make new commitments. The healing of long standing grievances was great.

"I am now participating in two prayer groups. One is an early morning men's group and the other is a Wednesday evening couples' group. Participating in these prayer groups is one of the things that keeps alive the feeling of renewal brought about by a lay witness mission.

"The Saturday morning coffee at a mission previously attended had the most meaning to me personally. It was during this session that a man prayed for me audibly and started a change in my life. The Saturday afternoon session of our mission was meaningful because it allowed me to learn some important things.

"I am thankful for the lay witness mission movement because it has changed my entire life. I have been able to start a quiet time with my wife and for the first time we study the Bible together and pray audibly for each other. As parents we have a new relationship with our six-year-old son and three-year-old daughter. Through family devotions and night time prayer they have learned conversational prayer and offer thanks and seek guidance from Jesus.

"My official church duties have taken on new meaning. I am now seeking to serve the Lord. The program of the church is a meaningful pleasure instead of a dull duty.

"For the first time in our lives my wife and I feel the need to tithe on our gross income. It has been rough going but we have faith in our future.

"My feeling and love for my fellowman have grown greatly. I can find something good and wonderful in everyone. I have empathy for the problems of others and have faith in the power of the Holy Spirit to make relationships right again.

"Through the power of prayer and the deep love experienced with the people of my prayer groups I have found a new strength to face my daily life. I have been able to rid myself of old prejudices and animosities. I have the courage and strength to witness, when an opportunity arises, to the power of Christ in my life. I have been able to relate to people with deep problems and needs and I have felt the power of the Holy Spirit in these endeavors. The greatest thing of all is lives changed by prayer.

"I have always been guilty of expecting my pastor to be perfect and above human emotions. I have come to realize that he is human and needs as much love and prayer as any layman. I can now respect and follow my pastor's leadership and at the same time love and support his personal weaknesses as he has always done for me.

"The friendships that have been found in Christian love and that have the bond of Jesus are the most beautiful and meaningful in my life.

"I am convinced that the lay witness mission is the greatest vehicle of initiating personal renewal in The United Methodist Church today."

THE PASTOR REPORTS

Where does the pastor begin? When did the spark begin to glow brighter? Was it in hearing fervent Christian witnesses? Was it in the books on small groups and renewal read and preached on?

All of these made their large imprint upon me as a person and a pastor. But perhaps most of all the credit should go to the witness of the witnesses with whom I've come in contact. Hearing their sincere testimonies moved me deeply. Seeing the deep changes taking place in the members of my own church has made a deep impression in my own life. This poker-faced preacher now oftentimes has misty eyes. My hidden tenderness is not always so hidden. My natural reticence has taken a beating. Unsuspecting airline passengers catch an earful as I eagerly share the good news. At the conference program council or other gatherings of the brethren I come in for much good-natured ribbing. "Don't ask Bob Main anything about lay witness missions or we'll be here all day."

My long-suffering congregation seems not to suffer quite so much, for the comment is often heard, "Say, hasn't Bob's preaching improved!" Whether it has or not I don't know, but at least their tolerance level has increased appreciably. Congregation and pastor alike are not so backward about sharing their respect and affection for each other.

I eagerly pray for my laymen as they depart for out-of-town missions and still more eagerly anticipate their return. Their good news of a great mission always carries me through several days of the week.

Can a pastor who has prepared his own heart, who has been prayed for by his people, who has felt their arms of support, be immune to the contagious joy of returning witnesses?

Perhaps I should go further to say that for the major portion of my life, both the formative years and the ministerial years, I have worked in the field of Christian education, in staff positions, as a college pastor, as a Wesley Foundation director, as a connectional officer. I have graduate degrees in the field of religious education and in the psychology of religion. My whole bent and inclination through the years has been to serve on conference boards of education and related boards. Evangelism would by nature have been my last choice of a conference board in which to serve. Yes, as a pastor I have pushed the evangelistic program of the church but at the same time felt more at ease in the field of education.

As a result of participation in all phases and facets of lay witness missions it has become much easier to do evangelistic work. Not all the uneasy feelings have been dispelled overnight but if I continue to draw encouragement from the laity of the church I shall hope to make further progress.

"Make a joyful noise to the Lord, all the lands! Serve the Lord with gladness! Come into his presence with singing!" (Psalms 100:1-2)

2

Missions in Three Other Churches

Paradise Hills

Because the pastor of Paradise Hills Church was one of the sources through which the New Mexico Conference came to know about lay witness missions and because his mission was a first for the conference we've asked him to summarize his mission. Comments from members of that church are reflected elsewhere in this book.

"While I was serving Linganore Methodist Church in Unionville, Maryland, I read an announcement of the conference workshop on evangelism to be held in Westminster, Maryland, in the summer of 1967. I attended only the Saturday session, but that was enough. I listened to Tap Hanson describe lay witness missions and I read the literature. I purchased several copies of *A Road to Renewal* to take home.

"Our commission on membership and evangelism was just beginning to study the book when we moved to New Mexico. As I began listening to the people of Paradise Hills Church, I realized that a mission would answer the prayers and the needs of many of us. The commission on membership and evangelism approved. There was a little difficulty at board meeting, but after listening to the preparation tape and further sharing, even those who were pessimistic agreed to go ahead. I was thrilled with the change one member made right in the meeting, a change from oppostion to agreement!

Already the mission was opening ways for Christ to work. And he did!

"The commission on membership and evangelism chose the committee chairmen and enlisted them. No one refused. We forgot to choose the general chairman for Paradise Hills, but God used this oversight to enable us to choose the best person. She and her husband have been going on missions ever since. Through the mission Christ has really made a difference in their lives.

"Preparation for the mission is very important. It is especially important that everyone pray earnestly for the mission. We were asked to pray that something good would happen to us and to our church.

"The mission exceeded our expectations. We planned for seventy-five on Friday night and had to set tables for one hundred! Many people were deeply touched by the wonderful, loving presence of our Lord.

"Sunday evening we discovered that we had one problem. At our evaluation we found out that one of the witnesses had been a little too pushy with one member. (I wrote concerning this to the coordinator.) At the evaluation session this member challenged the rest of us saying that the mission was too much like "holy rollers." The response of the rest indicated that a real change in them had taken place. They accepted what he had to say and continued to love him even though they could not agree with him. They went on to say that their experiences had been very real and were still real to them. This mission really opened the eyes of our people toward each other and toward their pastor. He is now a person instead of a preacher.

"We have four prayer groups going well, meeting each week. This includes one that meets Sunday mornings before services to pray with the pastor. This Sunday morning group idea has been suggested by our people wherever they go on missions. It means that much to them. It means a great deal to me. The idea came to me from a Baptist pastor in Maryland.

"Our finances are the best they've ever been. We have a sizable bank balance. The lights are on now at night on the front of the church. They were turned off a year ago because of lack of funds. One of the witnesses who came not only paid her way to come but left us a check for twenty-five dollars to help keep the lights on!

"We are beginning to investigate the Christian Growth Conference, hoping to have one soon. We are concerned that each person not only commit his life to Christ, but also discover his particular mission in life.

"Three couples and several youth have been going on missions ever since we had ours. One youth is planning to study for the ministry, leaning toward evangelistic work.

"Our faith in the mission at Paradise Hills has been well justified. I should say our faith in our Lord's willingness and eagerness to work through visiting lay men and women was well vindicated. One thing I would do next time would be to try to get more of the inactive members involved in the mission. How? I am not sure. Perhaps a better visitation and phoning program would help. Perhaps having some regulars go and get them would help."

Roswell First Church

The pastor of the 3,500 member First United Methodist Church of Roswell deserves a great deal of credit for helping to introduce missions to New Mexico. He had become acquainted with the movement at a meeting in Nashville.

He says, "I spent a year and a half getting our people to the point of understanding the great possibilities of a lay witness mission. After I had their interest we got the tapes, listened, discussed, and began diligently to follow the manual. We did everything we were supposed to do and even before the mission came around we were already having a rich experience.

"To be perfectly frank I did not know what to expect from the lay witness mission itself, but what we got was beyond any hopes we had concerning its possibilities.

"We were happy to make our mission a pilot mission and to invite other churches to send representatives to participate. We brought in many ministers and laymen, thus spreading the knowledge and interest in mission across our conference.

"Thirty witnesses from Georgia to California came to share with us. They came as strangers and left as friends. With their friendliness, their sincerity, and their openness they quickly won acceptance from our people.

"What a lift the mission has given my ministry. Things are not the same here at First Church. I'm not the same although I've always had some deep personal convictions concerning prayer and the Holy Spirit. Around me there have been many evidences of changed lives, of desires to become involved in renewal groups, and of greater community involvement."

El Paso First Church

Since the mission held at First United Methodist Church, El Paso was the first in that thriving border city, the first in a Texas church of the New Mexico Annual Conference, and fourth in the conference, we asked the pastor to tell us how he came to be involved in a mission, what some of his experiences were, and to answer some questions. The following paragraphs come directly from the pen of this long time conference leader whose mission was in late January of 1969.

"Word of mouth is still a very effective instrument for communicating the gospel. I first became aware of the lay witness mission through a laywoman of Abilene, Texas, where a most effective mission had been carried out in Aldersgate United Methodist Church. She was talking about it while visiting my mother-in-law. My wife and I questioned and probed deeply. The seed was planted. Then we began to hear more and more. When our conference board of evangelism indicated a pilot project for Roswell, New Mexico, we began to secure additional information.

"One of our own lay persons, who had some familiarity with missions and is a part of our commission on evangelism, was interested. Then we started giving thought to developing a date and planning for our own mission. As our interest and understanding grew we secured a tape from Lay Renewal Publications and this helped us gain further insight. We secured the book, *Road to Renewal,* and a little at a time, by use of the tape and other means of sharing, our council on ministries and our administrative board accepted the urging of our commission on evangelism. We were on the way to a tremendous experience, greater than we then imagined.

"Part of this was born because we were faced with a need for recommitment, renewal, and rededication. The preaching revival just didn't seem to have the answer for us. We needed a new voice and a new approach. We needed to know that our adults and our youth would be involved and would come out with a commitment that would make a real difference in their own lives. We knew, too, that we needed a confrontation that would permit an acceptance of an experience of Christ in the individual life.

"We are an older church, some eighty years of age. Many of our members have been active here for thirty or forty years. Forty-five per cent of our membership is over fifty-five years of age.

"We are situated in an inner-city location. We were not ministering to the neighborhood. We were an apathetic, complacent, but a spiritually hungry congregation.

"As we began to do our planning for the mission, we began to find a new zest in the people. The advance planning was of vital importance because it helped us to see what needed to be done, and began to get us deeply committed to the task. Praying for the mission is, without a doubt, one of the most effective preparations that can be done.

"There is no doubt that the Holy Spirit was strongly present and at work in the lives of our people, both before and during the mission. For some two or three weeks prior to the mission we began to feel a whole new atmosphere and attitude developing. It was easier to preach and easier to work, and easier to do a lot of the things that we needed to do.

"From Friday night right on through Sunday noon, there was an enlarging, growing feeling of the presence of Christ in our lives. By noon on Sunday there was a joy that could hardly be expressed, but was always making itself felt in many different places and ways. Some of our people having known each other over a long period of time, had just sort of accepted each other. But by Sunday noon they were confessing to each other their feelings, and openly seeking to enter into a warmer, more enjoyable relationship with each other. The Sunday night evaluation session was a tremendous experience. For more than two hours people continued to share openly some of the things they thought needed to happen as a result of the mission, and expressed some of the joys that had come to them. After we had formally dismissed there were still people who stayed around for another hour just talking and sharing, and reluctant to go home.

"We saw a lot of lives renewed, and a good many lives changed. We saw some attitudes changed vitally that have made a tremendous difference in the life of our whole church. One young couple from Puerto Rico had come to the place where they felt that this was not the church for them, and they had started looking elsewhere, but the weekend gave them the deepening that they wanted, and now they are assuming a very interesting and helpful relationship in our lives. We had a young Roman Catholic woman who had a tremendous desire for something other than that which she was getting in her spiritual life. Only a couple of weeks before the mission she had come into the membership of the church. Then as a sort of fringe benefit, in the Sunday school class she was attending, the witnesses, as they made their expression, really brought her to an experience of Christ in her own life. These are only a few of the things that have happened in our congregation as a result of the mission. In addition to this we are realizing more capabilities in a ministry that had been just sort of limping along.

"Committed laymen are sharing with me the services on Sundays. I have laymen who join together with me prior to going into the sanctuary for worship services, and we pray together. I have laymen who are volunteering for things where previously we could hardly get them to do any work. We are in the process of developing a new Sunday school class for young couples. We are getting more people involved in visitation to invite others to come with us to Christ. There seems to be a new willingness to volunteer to do the routine and sometimes unglamorous chores that have to be done to keep the wheels of our organization functioning. One of our men has gone far enough to volunteer to serve in an area where I didn't even suspect that we had anyone who might want to serve—the work area of ecumenical affairs. So, we find evidences of the growing earnestness of our people.

"There is still a need to evidence faith in our giving since this has been one area where we have yet to be willing to trust God to guide and provide. However, finances generally have been considerably ahead of the month prior to the mission.

"We also find there is a new anticipation in going out as witnesses to other missions. We now have about five prayer groups that came into being directly as a result of the mission. They are growing and strengthening. One of these is made up of our senior high and college-age teenagers, who are willingly attending a session at six o'clock on Wednesday mornings.

"But perhaps at this point, the most outstanding result of the mission is the deepening of faith in the lives of some of our people. In terms of really going out into a 'Mission to the World,' not too great an evidence has been seen. For the most part, it would seem to me that this is a 'talking experience' at this point. Perhaps at sometime during the weekend of the mission itself, some opportunity to discuss this area might be provided. There are some people who would object to too intense a push in this direction, but certainly it would be perfectly in order to give us some insights as to how we may 'go into all the world.' The actual outcome certainly ought to take place in the study groups and the prayer and sharing groups that come out of the mission, because it would then be an unimposed situation.

"However, some evidences of faith at work in the world are being seen. A scout troop has been begun as a part of the ministry to the neighborhood and people are more willing to participate in this work. We are moving now to develop a program for our single young adults—employed, military, and college. Other things that we had not been able to get under way before are now becoming realities.

"I had two things happen in my own life that are vitally important. I think my preaching has taken on a new dimension, and I know that there is, again, a deep search going on to find a more effective way of transmitting my faith through preaching. I found a renewed dedication, and certainly some of the resentments that had come into my life in the last two years were released, and I could work with a great deal more joy in my own work and with the laymen of our church.

"There has seemed to be little relationship between the mission and the social issues of the day. What enthusiasm there has been here is still evident and is strong among those who have always given concern to them. I notice that our youth especially see more need for reading of the Scriptures and for developing their prayer life, but have not yet gained insight into the involvement that comes in the social issues of the day. There has been evidence of bringing others into the fellowship, especially the prayer groups. Time and the Holy Spirit will tell.

"We have a new start as a part of the Body of Christ, and there is a new life among us. Yet I sense that there is a need for some means of continuing this enthusiasm and depth that it may spread and deepen. We have not yet found this as fully or as extensively as we might. It would be a contribution that might well be made if we could have some additional forms of follow-up, other than small groups, that would enlarge and continue the inflowing of the Spirit. It has been for us, though an experience through which we can come and shout, 'Hallelujah!' "

"O sing to the Lord a new song; sing to the Lord, all the earth! Sing to the Lord, bless his name; tell of his salvation from day to day. Declare his glory among the nations, his marvelous works among all the peoples!" (Psalms 96:1-3)

3

Reactions to the Missions

Views of Host Pastors

When a lay witness mission is held in a church the man probably most responsible for its being there is the pastor. It is a lay movement but a large measure of its success will be directly or indirectly due to the interest and work of the host pastor. Through some grapevine or official channel he has heard of a lay mission and he covets for his flock the same great experiences of others. At the same time he may have qualms about it all. He is anxious to know what kind of people are going to come his way; what his relationship with the coordinators is going to be; whether he can safely turn his people over to strangers and expect them to be all in one piece when it's over; what corner will he find himself backed into.

But in spite of these fleeting moments of doubt he proceeds to sell the idea to his people and to do the spade work necessary for a victorious mission. Of course he often has splendid help from "exposed" laymen in the sales job. But still he has to lay his reputation on the line for something quite new and strange.

When one minister wants to explore the possibilities of a mission and wants to clear up some uncertainties or some mental reservations he has, the people he wants to hear from first are the pastors who have hosted missions. And if he can hear from more than one the better. This is natural because he might expect Pastor Smith to go for "that sort of thing," but when Pastor Jones, who is the last guy in the world you would expect to be attracted to such a venture, speaks glowingly of a mission then a man has to really take notice.

So our proposal is to take a look at what a number of pastors in the Southwest have had to say after experiencing a mission of their own.

1. Since one of the worries of the host pastor is his relationship to the coordinator, let's look at some of the reactions.

From Central Church, Dalhart, "My relationship to our coordinator was very cordial. I had no difficulty turning the weekend over to him because I wanted this to be the fullest possible experience of Christ that it could be for my people."

The reply from Grace Church, Abilene, "My relationship to the coordinator was most cordial. He contributed much to my understanding of the mission. It was easy to turn it over to him. My doubts were dispelled."

One pastor had the advantage of previous acquaintance and said, "Our coordinator did an excellent job, and since he was a long time friend, I was able to turn the leadership over to him without qualms."

Another pastor reported the usual doubts about theology then concluded, "But after I met him and his wife I had no more doubts and it was easy to turn the weekend over to him when he came."

The pastor of Roswell First Church reported, "I had met and heard our coordinator so had no doubt in my mind concerning his ability. We had no doubts and were overjoyed and the results exceeded our expectations." He makes the point that we ought to have faith in the one who is to come because he would not be a coordinator and be given that position of responsibility had he not already passed the test.

The reply coming from New Haven Church, Tulsa, was, "It was easy to turn the weekend over to him."

2. Since firsthand eyewitness accounts are important and bear weight in a court of inquiry let's look at some of the reports about changed lives.

"I saw lives changed and deepened in a way that I had forgotten was possible."

"I think the lives of some of the members were changed and especially the young people are more spiritual."

"I saw lives changed and deepened in commitment. At least three men have gone out to witness with me and three have vowed to quit tobacco. One man who had not attended church in years was caught up in the power of a witness who stayed in his home and said to me, 'I must have what that young man has.' This man has not failed to attend a Sunday morning or night service since the mission."

"We did see a good number of people who were not only inspired and encouraged but also transformed. This was, of course, our main objective."

"Lives were changed during the mission and since."

"Yes, very definitely there was the evidence of changed lives, a sincere desire on the part of many to become involved in renewal groups."

3. In what activities of the mission did you feel the greatest impact, the greatest evidence of the Spirit working?

One felt that the small group meetings undoubtedly had the greatest impact and were the places where the Spirt worked most effectively.

Another who definitely felt the Holy Spirit present for his mission believed Saturday night was the highlight for the youth and the Sunday morning services for most of the people.

Still another believed that in the witnesses sharing and in the small group meetings the greatest impact of all was felt.

One responded that the presence and power of the Holy Spirit seemed to be evident from the first dinner meeting. "The immediate evidence of the Spiritual presence was in the atmosphere of love, not only on the part of our witnesses, but among our own people."

"I presume the greatest impact is to be found in the response within the lives of the people themselves and in the ease with which they talked about what was happening, the concern and the prayer, and the sharing in experiences."

One response came in these thoughtful words, "I think that the greatest impact of the mission came in the area of loving one's neighbor. People really began to see each other as real persons and to love and care for one another as they never had before. This became particularly evident Sunday evening at the evaluation session when one person voiced objections to the mission. Those who received the most in the mission did not reject the person who had raised objections, but told him they had experienced the reality of Christ. They said they could not agree with his objections but they still loved him. This would never have happened before the mission. Our Sunday night experience was great in that we met this challenge with love and with the sharing of our witness, without antagonism or argument. Yes, the Holy Spirit was strongly present and still is."

4. Did you feel that the Holy Spirit was strongly present and at work in the lives of your people during the mission?

"Our lay witness mission was the greatest outpouring of the Holy Spirit that I have ever witnessed."

"I definitely felt the Holy Spirit present for our mission."

"The Holy Spirit worked among our young people."

"The presence and power of the Holy Spirit was evident from the very first to the end."

"Yes, very definitely."

"Yes, the Holy Spirit was strongly present."

"No, but a stronger fellowship."

"Very much so. There was evidence on all sides. Nothing but the presence of the Holy Spirit could account for the things that were happening."

5. Did anyone on the fringe get caught up in the spirit of the mission?

"Yes."

"I feel that a few people on the fringe were caught up in the spirit."

"A few people on the fringe got caught up."

"Doubtful."

"Perhaps only a few, but oh, how great was the effect on their lives. It made the whole mission worthwhile."

Views of Adult Hosts

To determine something of the reaction of people in local

churches to the mission in their churches we asked a large number in some fifteen churches to respond to some questions about their experiences.

1. Tell how you felt getting ready for a mission.

The responses were varied—from indifference, to skepticism, to ignorance, to duty, to anticipation, to great excitement. These responses varied according to the degree the pastor and mission chairman had been able to sell the mission, and to the degree the people had entered into the spiritual preparation for the mission.

A Dalhart layman said, "I felt skeptical getting ready for the mission. I was a committee chairman and I went at the task with the misgivings that it was just another church project."

From Spearman came a woman's response, "We did not know what to expect so we just felt we were preparing for a revival or some similar meeting."

An Albuquerque man said, "I didn't think it would work," and his wife said, "I felt curiosity at first, then worry that it would flop. But I began to feel the warmness as I prayed for the mission."

An Abilene woman answered, "We wanted to push the panic button . . . thought it was too much to do in such a short time . . . people said they would help but didn't really want to . . . wondered why we had decided to have one."

An Alva teacher confessed, "We though it was just another revival under disguise . . . not too excited about it but willing to help the minister."

From El Paso this word, "I doubted that the members would participate."

An Alva layman said, "I was enthusiastic, but unable to comprehend the impact it might have on members of our church."

From Albuquerque, "I had a curious feeling and wanted more details of how this proposed thing weas going to work."

An El Paso man said, "I felt apprehensive. I knew something was going to happen, but couldn't anticipate just what it was."

A Roswell worker responded, "At first I felt totally alone, as if only my pastor and one other person really comprehended what was to take place."

From a young Albuquerque woman came this candid reply, "I was unconcerned and I did not anticipate our mission at Paradise Hills, nor did I take part in the preparation for the mission. I thought it would be stuffy and boring. We had planned to go on Friday night but had not planned definitely to go the remainder of the weekend—until the Friday night session was over, that is. We couldn't stay away after that."

"I prayed mightily that something would happen to our church and to me," replied an El Paso man.

"Great expectancy," was the short answer of a Crosbyton laywoman. Her husband said, "I was totally unprepared for the impact of the mission in our church. I was expecting something similar to the former renewal type services we had had. This one injected Jesus Christ into our congregation."

An Albuquerque woman, "I felt a tingling excitement and anticipation that 'good news' and a great experience were coming for the church, my family, and me personally. It started from the contagious spirit of the Paradise Hills laymen and built up through the 1:00 A.M. hour of the twenty-four hour prayer vigil with my son."

From Abilene came a woman's response, "When we were getting ready for the mission I had 'hope' to begin with that we 'might' have a good lay witness mission. Then as I began to pray for myself and others, really asking God to come into *my* heart and change *me* into what he would have me be—then I knew miracles were going to happen in all our hearts and lives in our church."

An Albuquerque woman said, "I was looking forward to the mission with great expectation. The pre-mission prayer groups helped to keep the anticipation alive."

A Spearman lady said she didn't know what the mission was really going to be but she prayed for it.

A native of Puerto Rico living in El Paso said, "I figured it was just another sort of convention. Boy, was I wrong . . .

I was about to leave our church to seek a warmer church but prayed and waited to see if the lay witness mission would change the church. Praise the Lord. It really did. Now I wouldn't change."

This word from Abilene, "In my life, I was hoping for a miracle. I had been working in the church for three years in numerous positions. I still felt unfilled and very miserable as far as my spiritual life was concerned. The week before the mission, I had a great experience in prayer. I felt for the first time that I was praying to God and he answered. However, I couldn't commit my life to Christ because I was afraid I would be expected to do something I couldn't handle. I had been doing that for three years and didn't like it. I went to the lay witness mission hoping for miracles and came home believing in them."

An Alva wheat farmer replied, "I did not know what it was all about but I was looking forward to finding out."

A retired army officer replied, "As I first started helping toward preparing for our mission I was a little hesitant about the whole matter. I did not have too much faith in the program. The nearer the time came though the better I began to feel about it."

A woman from Stinnett answered, "In getting ready for the mission, I felt mostly curiosity, along with a lot of others in our church. Everyone was asking, 'What are these people going to do?' and none of us really knew very much. But one thing I knew, I was very eager to find out. I had, not very long before that, had a wonderful experience with God which was already changing my life, but I had so much to learn, and a chance to hear others witness sounded like just what I wanted."

2. How did you feel at the Sunday night session?

Regardless of the feelings these people had in advance of the mission most were caught up in the contagion of the mission as evidenced by their witness concerning the Sunday night sharing sessions.

An enthusiastic Dalhart layman responded, "I went outwardly skeptical because I had boasted to a visiting witness that 'our church won't witness' but deep in my heart, which had been warmed at the morning service, I knew Sunday night would be different. And it was. Many people witnessed from the bottom of their hearts, and you could feel the presence of God in each of their lives."

From a Dalhart woman came this word, "On Sunday night I felt full of love and joy that the Holy Spirit had come into my life and the lives of so many of our church members."

A Spearman woman said, "At the evaluation session, I felt so full of love and happiness that I just wanted to laugh and cry at the same time. My Lord had never been more real to me or my friends so precious to me."

An Abilene woman replied, "I felt peace, joy, happiness, and was so thankful that God had answered so many prayers and was so thankful for the lay witness people that had been sent to us."

An Albuquerque woman said, "I could hardly wait my turn for a feeling of knowing that God had been in my presence all weekend. The Holy Spirit was evident everywhere."

A young housewife from Albuquerque reported, "On Sunday night I was filled with the excitement of my new love for Jesus Christ and more important, the realization of his love for me. I was amazed at the love that was felt by all in the sanctuary and by the feeling of oneness in Jesus Christ that we felt. For the first time in my life, I realized the importance of Christian fellowship."

In Crosbyton a lady said, "I felt truly close to the Lord and 'strangely warmed.'" Her husband added, "The Sunday night services seemed to draw our congregation closer to the Lord than any service we had ever had."

A minister's wife in Albuquerque said about Sunday night, "If not the highest, it was one of the highest moments in my entire Christian experience. I'm sure I felt God's presence and the Holy Spirit flowing in, through and around."

From Abilene came this comment, "Joy, joy, joy filled not only my soul but that of so many of our people. Sharing these joys and what Christ had done for us was joy unspeakable.

Oh, what a miracle happened in our youth group—that in itself was glory and joy enough for anybody."

From an Albuquerque nurse came this reply, "It was great to see that so many of us were willing to stand up and show our new love for Christ. I think back to it as one of my happiest moments."

An Albuquerque man replied, "The Sunday evening evaluation session was very meaningful. It was heartwarming to hear people be honest and make new commitments. The healing of long standing grievances was great."

An Albuquerque man, "It seemed as if Christ had touched everyone in our church."

A Dalhart couple admitted, "Sunday night we felt the power of the Holy Spirit and of prayer as testimonies of finding Christ, surrender to him, and requests for prayer were given. It was the most wonderful meeting we have ever been to and involved in."

From El Paso, "Our church wasn't the same church that night. All present were witnessing for the Lord. For the first time I felt my heart completely surrendered to the Lord."

This word from Abilene, "By Sunday night at the evaluation session, our church was a different place of worship. People I had known for three years were so filled with the Holy Spirit that it seemed I was meeting new friends. There were smiles on faces that hadn't smiled in months. People witnessed to what Jesus had meant in their lives and we knew they meant it. The people of our church were loving each other and sharing their lives with each other because God loved them."

From Tuscola, "One of my closest moments to God."

From Dalhart, "I was overjoyed. I had not expected this much response."

From Albuquerque, "Wonderful, really felt the Holy Spirit was in operation."

From Roswell this reply, "On Sunday night after the mission I was floating on cloud nine. I felt I had for the first time in my life really felt the presence of Christ inside me."

From Stinnett, "At our evaluation session I felt a buoyant,

joyous happiness, that was indescribable. It was wonderful hearing our own people witness, and to realize what those two days had done for all of us."

3. Are you participating in some kind of small group?

Every person responding indicated that they were participating in at least one group, and some in two and three. There were women's groups, couples' groups, youth groups and larger groups which broke into smaller groups. Discussion groups, Bible study groups, prayer and sharing groups were in evidence meeting early in the morning, at midmorning, at noon, and nighttime groups were meeting regularly, even six to nine months after missions.

4. Are you able to keep alive something of the feeling you had at the close of the mission?

Because the criticism so often leveled at revivals is that the glow soon wears off, this question was asked to determine if the results of a lay witness mission were more lasting.

The results were all in the affirmative but with some admitting it was a daily battle to find time to read, pray, and meditate. Some gave credit for their ability to keep the glow alive to their quiet time; others to their prayer group; and still others to their preparations for missions.

5. Would you share something of your joy and happiness with us? Were commitments deepened, resolves strengthened, loyalties straightened out? Has it helped your relationships?

An Albuquerque contractor in a hurry said, "Very, very much in answer to all these questions."

An Alva widow replied, "Yes. This has been a very hard year for me as I lost my husband. This mission has strengthened my love for God."

A Dalhart couple shared these beautiful words, "As for me, from the very beginning I felt a very real conviction that Christ was not in the center of my life. Though I had accepted him into my heart eighteen years ago, I had never given my life back to him to use as he saw fit nor had I asked him to guide me every day. I had an almost nil Bible study time and my prayer life was quite haphazard . . . these were made known to me so vividly through the power of the Holy Spirit that I could not resist my yielding all to him . . . My husband felt about the same way and now has turned the management of his life and business over to Christ. We had a very happy home and marriage but it is even better now that we are back to daily devotions. We go to church with a new interest and with a love for Christ and his people. Our daily life is in better order—problems are brought before him—peace is felt."

From a Spearman teacher came this word, "The joy and happiness I have found since our lay witness mission is the result of faith and renewed awareness of God's love. I feel closer to my husband and two-and one-half year-old daughter because I more fully recognize the blessings they are to me. Our friendships are deeper because we now share our love of God with many of our best friends. My schoolteaching is more meaningful because I can now depend on God's help in my preparation and in my classroom. All in all, life has more meaning, more purpose than ever before."

A positive response came from an Abilene housewife, "Our commitments are indeed deeper, our resolves strengthened, our loyalties deeper. It has helped to straighten out our faith, to make us more concerned about our fellowman. It has made us want to be a witness at work each day and we have tried to do so."

From Dalhart a housewife reports, "There is a deep inner joy and peace in my life. I am having a daily quiet time and prayer time. I have a better understanding of my husband and a better sharing of our religious life. I have more love for people in the church and feel a new relationship in sharing Christ's love." Her husband says, "Although I had made a full commitment about twelve years ago, and had prospered in my business and was very happy, there did seem to be something missing. I wondered why I wasn't on fire as were John Wesley, Francis Asbury, and some of the earlier Christians. I believe the Holy Spirit came into my life for real. And by practicing the daily quiet time the 'let down' has been slight. In fact so many things are happening in our small town that we are being inspired all over again."

Already pictured by his pastor as a staunch and dependable churchman a Dalhart man now says, "The joy and happiness that I have shared is enormous. I have a different outlook with my teenage sons and my wife. My wife and I say 'I love you' to each other in the mornings again. We hug and kiss our boys at bedtime, and share a prayer time with them. I feel differently toward my business associates and employees . . . In my quiet time each morning, which I am having for the first time in my life, I feel quite good, a sincere feeling of calmness is in my life . . . I feel that I am getting a glimpse of Christ for the first time. My resolves were strengthened, and when they weaken, it is easy to get back in line by asking Christ's help. Ask and it is there. I have had the URGE to witness to my fellowman. I have been to the home of an invalid that I had been thinking about and prayed for him and with him, and this is something that I had not done before. The most remarkable thing about this is that it is easy for me to talk about Christ to other people, where before it was unheard of."

An Albuquerque teacher says, "My commitments are deeper. I feel a sense of duty, loyalty, and closer relationships with my friends and my fellow church members as well as in my neighborhood that I never had before."

From El Paso a man has this to say, "The mission has meant a whole new life for me and my family. At home we join in family prayer at least twice daily. This is a completely new experience for us. At work I have caught myself witnessing to people I would not have thought about mentioning Christ to before. I now have a completely different outlook on church. For the first time in my life I really look forward to going to church and participating in all activities."

From Albuquerque, "It has not solved all my problems, but has given me strength to rely on God's judgment and guidance in those areas that are 'under reconstruction' or needing help."

Another El Paso man said, "I am so thankful I attended each meeting. I now tithe and find it a pleasure. It helped my home life, and strengthened my resolves to do better."

From a Crosbyton mother comes this word, "My husband and I had been in a prayer group of mixed denominations for two years and had received joy unspeakable and blessings I would define comparable to a lay witness mission outgrowth. Therefore it was most refreshing and encouraging for this to happen to our own church, to give us a kindred feeling with those with whom we share our experiences. I think God deals with us individually as we open our lives to him. We were drawn to him through a healing need in a young son, and through this searching and healing, found a life abundant. It does not go away as some are afraid after a lay witness mission. He makes life worth living at home, church, and work. It is a complete 'new' life, and commitments, service and just living fall into place."

In Albuquerque a man reports, "It is a gratifying feeling when you realize that the Holy Spirit has been at work in your life and you anticipate even greater blessings in the work of his Kingdom." And his wife adds, "As a result of the mission in our church, I have been given a new perception into all areas of my life. I know that the Lord is interested in all that I do. It is so much easier to pray and feel the pressure of the Holy Spirit. I am able to love people more."

From Roswell, "As a result of the lay witness mission I feel I have completely given myself to Christ. Now I enjoy what I do at the church whereas before I did it as an obligation and felt it was expected of me. It has been very meaningful to me and my wife to pray aloud together for the first time in our married life. We have never had any particular trouble in our marriage but praying together seems to deepen our love for each other even more. Also as a result of the mission my wife and I have started tithing. We had increased our contributions in recent years but never before to a complete tithe."

From Stinnett, "It would be hard for me to tell you just how much this mission has meant to me. I was moving so slowly in my spiritual growth since God had become so close to me, and I was not satisfied, but just did not know much about how to get on with witnessing, as I had been very timid about talking to people. Well, that weekend just seemed to give me a big shove in the right direction. I started witnessing during those days, and have found it no problem since then. It has brought about a much more wonderful relationship between me and my husband. He went to the mission only because I wanted him to, but after the first night I did not even have to urge him, and he now attends the couples' group regularly with me, and takes an active part."

6. Any other comments would be appreciated.

Real warmth crept out of the letters at this point. A sampling of comments is as follows:

"I don't want to be a radical but yet I want to let people know about the wonderful love Christ has for all of us even when we fail him and he is so ready to forgive and let us try again."

"As a result of our lay witness mission we have a 'new church.' It is a wonderful feeling to go and share blessings and receive new ones—so many more than I ever thought possible. There is a new interest in Sunday School, in listening to our pastor and in simply going to Christ's church. My husband and I are so grateful for what it did for us in our own lives and now we are willing to become 'pipelines for Christ and not just storage tanks.' "

"We've had many revivals in our church but have never had a meeting with the impact of this. We've discussed this, and decided it was because these people came to us out of love and that they are just lay people as we are. They so strengthened our desire for prayer and study that this in turn will strengthen our church, town, and all we touch. This is our fervent prayer."

"I feel that God has been working in my life for a long time. I'm thankful that he never let or left me alone. He let me have my own way and rediscover him as I would. I have not by any means arrived but thanks to him I am growing in his love and grace."

"I have experienced nothing in this difficult day for churches and families which seemed to be the answer to problems as has the lay witness mission. The realization that without the

Holy Spirit I am nothing, the church and its influence is nothing, has meant everything to me."

"I am very thankful to God for this lay witness movement in Methodist churches. I feel people are hungry for a reality as they have never been before. God is moving by his Spirit, and it is very thrilling to be a part of this, or even to be living in such a time. I personally believe hearts are hungry to receive the baptism by Jesus with his Holy Spirit. I definitely feel this will have to come before a person will be satisfied or before he will find his fulfillment in life."

"We need to know how to help those that were not able to take part to feel a part of us now without saying too much to cause hard feelings."

"I have decided that God is even present when one is sinning and that he will surely forgive me if I only ask, but I must make an effort to do better. I must pray more and be more honest with God in order to feel his love."

"A lay witness mission has meant more than any revival, spiritual life mission or any other Christian experience that has entered our church. If only there were a way to continue the 'glow' for a long period of time—or get more people involved—in other words to see it GROW."

"It was the greatest thing that has ever happened to me, my family, or our church. People are praying, they are seeing the results, and many things are happening for the good of the Lord. I cannot recommend the lay witness mission highly enough."

"When we get home at night our family reads from all the good books suggested by the mission and from *Good News for Modern Man*. We have given many copies away to friends and relatives. It is a glorious feeling to read and share what you have read."

"In the two weeks since our lay witness mission so many things have happened that prove the Holy Spirit is working in our church and in my own life. Of course I've believed for many years that God was better at handling finances than I was. But I now know there are things he really would like us to have if we could only put ourselves in a position to receive.

For a couple of years I had debated about whether to buy a new airplane. I could afford it but it seemed such a waste of money. After the mission I began to pray. Then as if in answer to prayer I found a slightly used plane just forty miles from home. I will be flying a plane load of witnesses to Ft. Worth the latter part of this month."

"I sincerely believe the lay witness missions are the future of the church. Nothing could be more effective than sincere, loving laymen who really care about their fellowmen."

"At our El Paso mission one of the witnesses and I made a pact to pray for each other's brother. I had a brother, with seven children, who had been out of work for several months. The witness had a brother who had not yet found the Lord. Some two or three weeks later I heard from my mother that my brother had found a job. The next day I heard from the witness that his brother had gone at 2:00 A.M., after a party, to see a minister. At 5:00 A.M. he left after completely surrendering himself to the Lord. That is how wonderful our Lord is. This experience has deepened my faith and my loyalties and helped me greatly at home and at work."

A Dalhart man testifies, "I feel the lay witness mission can awaken the twentieth century church. The Holy Spirit moved through the witnesses who visited our church. We are grateful for his presence."

From Alva, "We were happy to see a number of young people becoming interested. Both youth groups have increased in membership. Two young people have been asked to go out on a lay witness mission."

Views of Youth Hosts

Because young people have been responding so enthusiastically to lay witness missions we will share with you some of their thoughts as they approached a mission and as they concluded one. Their honesty is refreshing and their resulting witness is thrilling to hear.

Below is a sampling of their responses to several questions.

1. What were your feelings as you looked forward to having a mission in your own church?

"I thought it was just another 'one of those.' "

"I wasn't sure I could stand up to people and really get anything out of it."

"I did not belong to the church at the time of the mission but my feelings at first were of indifference."

"Not very interested."

"My feelings as I looked forward to having a mission in my church were terrible. I didn't want one. I had my weekend all planned and that was all messed up. And to top it all off I was going to have one of the people staying in my home."

"I didn't prepare for it."

"As our mission approached I looked on it as an obligation or a duty that I was required to perform because I had no choice. I felt that the lay witness mission would ruin the weekend and nothing more. Self, who at that time ruled my life, was looking at the mission and constantly telling me that my present life was best."

"In looking forward to having our lay witness mission I didn't know what exactly what to do. I was told that I would have a team member stay with me. I was like everyone else, thinking that a team member was a 'short, fat, goggle-eyed' person who knew the Bible from cover to cover, and turned to a certain passage for answers every time he or she was asked a question."

"I looked forward to our mission with a high degree of excitement."

In answer to question two the reactions of these same young people give an idea of changes taking place in attitudes during the mission.

2. What part of the mission seemed to mean the most to you?

"I started to open up Saturday night, but I feel Sunday meant the most."

"The Saturday night experience."

"The part I liked most was the sharing groups after we had heard the witnessing."

"The most significant part of the mission for me came Saturday night. We split into four small groups, and there

I finally was able to admit my needs in front of the group. They prayed for me, and I felt a strength that heretofore I had lacked."

"The small group discussion meant the most to me."

"The part of the mission that meant the most to me was the prayer chair. We all went to the prayer chair and gave our lives to our Lord and Savior."

"My interest steadily progressed as the mission went along. Sunday morning was the climax for me. As I went to the altar my heart was pounding and my eyes were full of tears. I had never before felt the presence of God so strongly as I did then, except perhaps at the prayer chair the night before. This was different though, my sins had already been forgiven and I was giving my life to Christ and he has never let go. I have slipped several times, but he's always there whenever I ask for something. The congregation was singing 'Have Thine Own Way, Lord' and the song has never been the same to me since. Every time I hear it now, my eyes fill with tears. It's almost as if that hymn is a prayer, a commitment I have to Jesus Christ."

3. Was the weekend of your mission a real growth experience for you?

"Yes. I am closer to God, and I, too, am witnessing."

"Yes, it helped me to grow spiritually and also to gain faith."

"No, the weekend of my mission was not a growth experience for me. I was 'reborn' and had to start over again."

"The weekend of our mission was the greatest growth experience of my life. It changed my life completely, and started me on the road toward Jesus Christ. I feel that the mission was not only a growth experience but a transformation too."

"The weekend of our mission was a real growth experience for me. Our youth group was getting very bad. It seemed that we couldn't agree on anything. I'll have to admit, I was one of the fighters, and was very disagreeable also."

"I grew in many ways that weekend. I grew spiritually because for the first time in my life I really had faith in Jesus Christ as my personal Savior. I grew in love because for the first time I knew the awesome power of it. I grew in wisdom because I began to realize the really important things in life. The mission really changed my life because it gave me a set of goals unachievable without the help of Jesus Christ himself, but goals that I am striving to reach."

"Yes, I came to a greater understanding of my purpose as a Christian. I saw the wonderful way in which God can melt the hearts of people with his eternal love and remold them, making them truly one in Christ Jesus. It was and is fantastic and of course could only be accomplished by the grace of our Father."

4. Is there anything else you would like to share with us about feelings at the mission and since that time?

"After the late service on Sunday morning I felt like hugging myself and anyone that was near, and running and jumping like a kid! I guess I was a kid in a sense—after all I had experienced the rebirth that's mentioned in the Bible. Since the mission, I have lost the childlike feeling, but what has replaced it is just as good. I have a feeling of peace. I feel like I don't need to worry anymore and that God is with me and he is handling my life so that I don't need to worry. Also, I can try a little harder now, and it's a little easier for me to accept people without condemning them."

"God changed my life in a lay witness mission and I now have a stronger channel of communication with God and Christ."

"I think the lay witness missions are great. I personally feel they are better than revivals, and should be used in their place. Our church has had many revivals and the feeling has lasted a week or two, but the lay witness missions better meet our needs and have more lasting results."

"I wish I could express my feelings like they actually were at the mission. I had such a feeling of faith, love and joy that my entire life has been changed. I'm an entirely different person now, even eight months later. I have a dependence on the Lord, through prayer, I never had before. Lay witness missions, in my opinion, have the power to change the nation if they can spread fast enough."

"The youth made me think of the early Methodist evangelists in colonial times who traveled the country sharing their witness. I think an effective follow-up should be planned so that people will stay interested, involved, and continue growing."

"And a vision appeared to Paul in the night: a man of Macedonia was standing beseeching him and saying, 'Come over to Macedonia and help us.' " (Acts 16:9)

4

Attitudes of Participants

The Coordinators

A coordinator comes to his position as a committed individual and as one who usually has had lots of experience as a witness. He has followed the field of service long enough to be both subjective and objective about his missions.

Because this report is in a real sense a report of moods, feelings, and experiences, and the movement of the Holy Spirit in people's lives we asked men from the Southwest to record their impressions on some phases of a mission.

1. At what other sessions besides the team sessions does the Holy Spirit seem to be most evident?

Responses here vary from leader to leader and from church to church, indicating that the Spirit works in many ways to reach the hearts of people. One believes he has seen the presence of the Spirit more in the small groups on Saturday night, "This seems to be the time when more people have had time to examine the very content of their lives and begin to let God stir in them."

Another believes also that the work of the Holy Spirit is most evident in the small group meetings. "Again, here the format seems so simple that the fantastic results which are seen must be accredited to the miraculous working of the Holy Spirit."

In responding another leader had these perceptive things to say, "The depth of the Friday night sessions depends on the willingness of the host congregation to shed their mask and get down to their real needs, hungers, and longings. But the Holy Spirit becomes more evident as a mission grows. After a night for thinking, the coffees on Saturday provide the first real chance to step out for spiritual food. The events of Friday and Saturday nights, unseen and often unheralded, produce the most profound Christian growth and adventure in the entire mission. Evidences of rebirth of the hard core members of the congregation become evident on Saturday night as the small groups dismiss to go to the altar. Some people have not been back to the altar since they were married."

A very experienced Texas coordinator says, "I believe that the Holy Spirit is always present when someone is witnessing about what Jesus Christ means to his or her life. The Holy Spirit is much at work in the sharing groups as people become vulnerable to each other as they share their feelings. But I believe the Holy Spirit is most evident at the Sunday evening services after the visitors have left and the local people begin to share their love of Christ and each other. I have seen old enmities destroyed and a new love take its place. I have seen grown men crying and hugging each other and apologizing for past wrongs and begging forgiveness. I have seen stiffnecked, uncompromising men become pliable and usable at these Sunday evening sessions."

2. In the midst of your chores as a coordinator do you still get caught up in the fervency of the mission?

The replies of these men give us confidence and assurance that they have not become calloused or self-satisfied in their leadership role.

One says, "To me there seems to be no way that a coordinator will not be caught up considering the many life-changing experiences, the abounding feeling of brotherly love, and the miraculous answers to prayer on every hand through the work of the Holy Spirit."

A second one says, "Missions have been another way in which the Holy Spirit has worked in my life to keep me reminded that I am truly dependent in all things upon its power, and thus, to more or less force me to keep my life disciplined to his way."

Another veteran leader reports, "We get caught up in the fervency of the lay witness mission when we are packing our traveling bags at home. We plan to discontinue participation in lay witness missions when we fail to thrill at the prospect of witnessing for Jesus Christ."

Still another confesses, "As the mission progresses, and the signs of surrender and love begin to show, I find myself beginning to enter into the race to victory at the altar Sunday morning."

3. Which part of a mission seems to be the most productive in terms of hoped-for results?

Here we got varied responses as the leaders interpreted the question in different ways.

One says you cannot be sure until you begin to hear the scattered reports about people and their activities after they have settled down to the routine of life again. The one thing all the witnesses are hoping for is renewed lives. "When we begin to hear how people are having a daily quiet time, how they are gathering together for weekly prayer meetings and sharing times, when we hear of activities they have undertaken as a service to our Lord—these are the areas where results are the most meaningful in terms of hoped-for results. A changed life, a new relationship in a near-broken home . . . these things make our cups run over."

Another coordinator responded, "In thinking back over the missions I have participated in, I am unable to say that any one part is more productive than others. As I look back, however, it seems that those people who have been stimulated to continue in the small group atmosphere are the ones who have continued to grow 'in the unity of the faith and of the knowledge of the Son of God.' I am sure this must be our most hoped for result of any mission."

A third leader declares that the small group is the most productive of results, that in spite of the colorful formal witness the small group is where things happen.

A fourth person pointed out that when the host congregation prayed for each other's expressed needs and desires, that all leaders experienced great fulfillment. "This is true church renewal for this is the ministering of saints to saints. People have begun to shuck their own burdens for those of others. Christ takes our burdens and we take the loads of others."

Still another leader says, "The whole mission blends together to produce the results that we pray are God's will for the church, each individual and the pastor. We hope of course that small renewal groups will be one of the outgrowths of each mission. This is where the continued renewal takes place in the life of the individual and the corporate body of Christ. It is also hoped that each person whose life has been touched will start a personal study and devotional life so that he may continue to grow in the faith and knowledge of the Lord Jesus Christ."

4. Any other thoughts to share?

"Lay witnesses are just everyday people who show through their experience how the reality of salvation and the work of the Spirit changed their lives."

Another expressed a humble but sincere desire to continue to mature spiritually. "I want to take a new step each time because I can't allow myself to feed off the experiences of other people as I observe them. Growth must be my own as a result of my daily walk with God . . . I am thrilled that he has used me in the manner that he has and I want to continue to be used day by day. The only way I can be effective is to grow a bit every day. Since I get to see so many great Christians working in these missions and in the churches we visit, I find myself wanting to try to know just a little bit more about God each day. As a direct result of my work as a coordinator, I have found that if I am to be an effective leader, I must plant myself on firm spiritual ground."

A third man shared this intimate feeling with us, "What more can I say than I met my personal Savior and Lord as a result of the lay witness program. My mother and father did the same. My brother and wife did the same. Without trying to convince anyone of my previous condition before my rebirth, my testimony was put in a nutshell by my host in a Mississippi town. 'At the altar of his church he sobbed aloud.'

I have held every office in this church from Sunday School up and this morning at age forty, I met him for the first time."

Adult Witnesses

We have been seeking in this report to look at the lay witness mission from many angles and many viewpoints. We have seen it through the eyes of local pastor, local adults, and local youth who were on the receiving end of the experience from the viewpoint of those who both gave and received. The adult witnesses gave of their time and their money. But most of all they gave of themselves. They clarified their own thinking, grew spiritually in the team sessions and in the sharing sessions, and came away with a host of new friends.

Their responses to some queries put to them indicate that their respective missions were in good hands. Regardless of their secular position in life they came to their first mission mostly as babes in the woods.

"I was scared, didn't know what I would say. Why did the Lord need me?" asked a Tuscola, Texas man.

A woman from Spearman reported herself to be both eager and apprehensive. "I was afraid I would not know what to say and so I knew I was looking for a greater experience for myself and I wondered if I was being hypocritical to try to share with someone else an experience I was not mature in."

A music teacher from Roswell replied, "I really did not know whether I wanted to go or not, my wife having been the deserving one. Truthfully I was afraid and did not know what to expect."

A nurse from Albuquerque puts it this way, "There was excitement but also some apprehension. It never has been easy for me to speak before an audience."

A technician reports, "I was very nervous the first time I prepared to be a witness on a mission. I did not feel adequate or up to the task. I went on faith that maybe I could help someone as I was helped in a mission."

A teacher joins the others in reporting, "I felt a sense of inadequacy and great humility and need of Christ's presence if I were to be effective and yet a tingling excitement and anticipation—a prayer answered for I felt I *had to go."*

A woman from Spearman felt like getting ready for a revival and husband says, "Frightened."

"I guess I felt very humble that someone thought I was ready to go on a mission. I felt very inadequate," replied another woman.

One put it simply, "Deep heart-searching humility."

An insurance man responded, "There was a complete feeling of inadequacy. It took a lot of prayer to make that trip. I really had to turn that over to God."

An Albuquerque man put it this way, "Afraid I wouldn't do things right," and his wife reported, "I felt fear. I hadn't learned confidence in God yet."

A Tulsan confessed, "As I prepared for my first mission I thought how inadequate I was for the task ahead. I went to Jesus in prayer and for help and guidance. He got me out of the way and used me as he saw fit."

"The excitement of a new adventure," responded a Dallas layman.

This word from an Irving woman, "I had a fear of being inadequate and a flop. I wondered how I ever agreed to go in the first place. My husband was also concerned about the validity of his witness and had just plain cold feet—but still wanted to go and share."

From Yuma came the answer, "I was somewhat fearful of being able to do God's work, although a propelling force was urging me forward. I felt that my witness was not adequate. However, the knowledge that God would speak through me became a joy I could not resist."

But with one mission behind them the witnesses began to feel a little more confidence as they anticipated subsequent missions. The eagerness and excitement were still there, but now they knew they would receive a fine welcome wherever they went and that the people for the most part would respond to their help. Having seen wonderful things happen they were anxious to see them again. And having found where they were lacking in their own preparation they have been doing their homework better. And having grown themselves during their first mission they approach the second with a feeling of being better able to cope with whatever may come. They have a greater reliance on the work of the Spirit in what they do. Here are some of their shared feelings.

"I couldn't wait to get there."

"I am eager to go. I know that God will be with me and I do not worry about saying the wrong thing for he can use any effort in his behalf. I still seek to grow spiritually through the other team members, but I know now that even the greatest Christians are not perfect and only as I give what small faith I have will it truly grow."

"I went better prepared. I thought about my witness, wrote down some of the things about my life that I felt God wanted me to share and then prayed about each one, asking God if I was being honest with myself and with him. He showed me where I was wrong and what I could change. When the time came for me to witness I was calm, and felt his presence so strongly I was able to witness with a joy in my heart that I never knew before. I don't think I have ever enjoyed anything so much."

"Much anticipation for what I could gain through encouragement of others and what the local people could see and feel . . . the spirit of Christ working through men and women just like themselves."

"The preparation for subsequent missions has been easier and more joyful but there is still a tinge of uneasiness prior to each mission. This is an honest feeling of concern about being inadequate and unworthy."

"When I was asked to go on subsequent missions I had to pray for guidance that I could be used for his glory and not my own."

"I still feel humble and inadequate but I now know a bit more what to expect."

"Great joy and desire to be completely used of the Lord—also joy of fellowship with other believers."

"I had more faith that God would see me through the second one."

"I felt the Lord had sent me there to help someone."

"Still a feeling of inadequacy, but at the same time an abiding knowledge that God would use me if I trusted him. I went feeling very concerned about small group work, yet knowing the Holy Spirit would be there and that he would lead. I still look forward to going."

"I felt a tremendous joy at the thought of participating in other missions. It seemed I was doing that which Jesus commissioned us to do, to 'go ye and make disciples. . . .' "

Some answers to the question, "What part of the mission means the most to you?" were:

"Team sessions and small groups."

"I enjoy the fellowship and meeting new people who immediately love and accept me the most."

"The team sessions set the stage, bring the group together, and make us acutely aware of God's presence and his power."

"First, the small group meetings after the evening witnessing; coming a close second are the team sessions."

"The team sessions I believe are very fertile fields for the Holy Spirit. There is a oneness of hearts and minds. You feel the love flowing from one to another."

"The small group sessions are the most meaningful part of the mission to me as a witness. The local people always open up and communicate with each other as they have never done before."

"The team sessions meant more to me spiritually and I would say the small group meetings were a close second. It was a marvelous experience to see people open their hearts to us and reveal their hopes and fears to complete strangers."

"Ministering to those present—group sessions and prayer fellowships."

"The team sessions with the exciting reports of what is happening to the youth."

"Small group discussions."

"Team sessions and ladies' luncheons. Perhaps because the luncheon is the only time where women can really share in their problems of being Christian wives and mothers."

"What part of the mission seems to be most productive in

producing changed lives and warmed hearts?" received these responses.

"Small group discussions."

"I believe it all works together in a way to produce the results suggested. It is a process of growth throughout the weekend with all parts necessary."

"Let me say that the sum total of the entire weekend is a mountain-top experience with the Lord."

"The most productive part is the morning worship hour; but this is also due to the weekend as a whole and the impact that the total mission has had on the local members."

"Praying for individuals by name. Sharing your witness. New growth and love for them."

"It would be hard to say which part of a mission changes lives and warms hearts most. Every individual responds differently to each part of a mission. I firmly believe that if a person will attend a lay witness mission with an open and seeking heart that sometime during the weekend he will identify with some aspect so that he will want to start something new in life."

"The small groups at night and Sunday morning final service."

"This is unpredictable and not uniform."

"Sometimes in the prayer fellowships, or most certainly at dedication time on Sunday mornings."

"It seemed to take the entire program. Some hold back from session to session. Some seem to respond immediately. Not any one session could have produced the response that came at the Sunday morning service."

"The Saturday coffee and the Saturday night small group session seem to be most productive."

"Saturday evening groups and Sunday morning services are the 'harvest' of the weekend."

In answer to requests for other comments the witnesses might have these replies are typical:

"A man came to Albuquerque and helped start a new life for me. I will continue to try and do the same for others."

"Knowing that you are going to be called on to witness

before men about your faith in God causes you to search your soul more, to pray more, to study more, in general to clean up and put in order your life. You can't get by with saying 'Here's what you should do,' but must be able to say, 'Here's what I do to have a working relationship with Christ . . . it works for me . . . how about you?' You can't be a phony."

"It seems in all honesty that going as a lay witness gives me the most exciting opportunities, since I gave my life to full-time Christian service, to express and tell and share my deeper feelings and convictions about what Christ means in my life and what he should mean in our churches and in the world."

"God loves you and I love you is the good news. Isn't it wonderful that so many people are discovering this?"

"I'm so grateful for this lay renewal and eager to help in its continued growth."

"My experience indicated that the lay witness program is being received much better by the laymen than the pastors."

"I think the lay witness movement is one of the greatest things that has happened in The United Methodist Church. I wish I could be a really effective witness and had the time and money to go on more missions."

"My concern is following up with the people that I am sensitive to. How does one encourage and help them to continue to grow in their religious life, especially the young people who do not have a lot of religious background?"

"Do not be careless with this movement. Do not *program* the Holy Spirit as liberal writers have done. Let the clergy accept the fact that laymen can lead others in his church to Christ."

"God loves you and I love you. I could not always look my brothers and sisters in the face and say this with a deep rich meaning, but now I can. Thank the Lord."

"My whole life has improved—at home, at work, at church. This truly has been a great adventure with the Lord."

"I feel it has been one of the most fruitful avenues of service that God has given me. I would suggest that an effort be made, as soon as possible, after each mission to incorporate interested people in subsequent lay witness teams before their enthusiasm dies and they are tempted to decline."

"Tremendous movement—brings the role of the laymen back to the role he had in the first century. If anything can restore Methodism to being an evangelical force, this will. Wonderful opportunity for whole families to share a common goal—no generation gap. Movement could stand much more emphasis on youth. Makes you, as an individual, think through your witness when you realize the responsibility that is yours."

"At first I wanted to see progress, but as I came to know my God I forgot about progress and concentrated more on the work at hand. I realized that the seeds were being planted and God would water them and make the sun to shine upon them. Into each life something beautiful would grow. I knew I was there in the service of my Lord and someone would hear my witness, some one whom God had chosen to be there, and I thank God."

Youth Witnesses

Since high school and college youth are too busy to fill out long questionnaires, no matter what their good intentions might be, we have asked only a few questions. Noted here are a few representative answers which will give the flavor of the experiences involved .

1. What were your feelings as you prepared for your first mission?

"I looked forward to the mission with a high degree of excitement."

"As I prepared for my first mission I was very unsure of myself and talked to God a lot about it."

"Scared."

"My feelings as I prepared for my first mission were mixed. I was scared, but I knew God would be with me. I did not want to go, but I wanted to tell people my story. Boy, am I glad I went, I loved it."

2. What part of the mission means the most to you?

"The team sessions and the prayer chair on Saturday night always mean the most to me. It always means a lot to me when the person I stay with accepts Christ for the first time in his life."

"The last night when the youth, using the prayer chair, pray together and for each other, is the most meaningful. It is amazing what God can do with people when they pray."

"Saturday night when the altar of the church is open for anyone."

"The close fellowship with God and people."

"The small groups and the Saturday night session are the most meaningful for me."

"I think the most meaningful part of the whole mission is still the Sunday morning service, but only because of what preceded it."

3. Have your experiences as a witness been real growth experiences for you? Can you put it into words?

"It has been a real experience to me. I always realized that I had another part of my life that I had been keeping for me. Sometimes it often seems like receiving Christ for the first time, but this is just giving over more of my life. I always come home with more than I take."

"Each time that I witness, I grow a little more in faith and strength and these missions give such a sensational opportunity for witnessing that I naturally grow."

"Yes, my experiences as a witness have helped a lot in my growth. My spiritual life is not so separated from my physical life as it was before. I have been able to live with Christ more of the time. Many problems could not have been solved without his help. I still wish I could live with Christ all of the time. I am working on it though and with his help I can. I wish I could tell all of the ways my life has changed but they are far too numerous. The best statement I can make is that Christ is growing more and more into my daily life, and I know he will continue as long as I let him."

"First, from the mission program I began a self-examination of my own life. This was the beginning, for as I began to see myself as I really was, I was able to spot needs, fears, and problems that were present in my life. Second, the mission introduced me to a group of people who had needs, fears, and problems like mine. But these people went a step further, they confessed their needs, while I 'hid mine in my heart.' As I continued to keep my needs and fears to myself there came great frustration and a longing to be set free. Finally, I realized that my true identity was being overrun by the person others wanted me to be and by an impostor self-made image. Out of need, the Gospels and words of Christ began to make sense. 'I came that you might have life and have it more abundantly.' Jesus gave me a life to live and he lives in me. The lay mission has encouraged me to grow in Christ. My acceptance of Jesus Christ as Lord of my life was but a beginning to a daily adventure as I began to follow him in everyday living. I have heard the charge that the lay witness mission is a shallow channel in which people are witnessing to only one experience. I disagree, for in the missions I have participated in there have been witnesses who always had something fresh and vital to share not only in regard to first acceptance but also growth. Through the sharing of my witness, I find two basic needs met. First, I am able to fulfill the words of Christ when he said, 'ye shall be my witnesses.' Second, I am able to see through my witness how God is really shaping and molding my life as he would have it to be. This recall surely adds strength to my faith. When I gave my life to Christ, I asked him to make me the person he wanted me to be—you know, he is doing just that."

"As he walked by the Sea of Galilee, he saw two brothers, Simon who is called Peter and Andrew his brother, casting a net into the sea; for they were fishermen. And he said to them, 'Follow me, and I will make you fishers of men.' Immediately they left their nets and followed him." (Matthew 4:18-20)

5
Understanding How a Mission Functions

Role of Host Pastor

The host pastor is very much involved in the preparation of a mission. Once he has sold his people on the need to have a mission and a mission has been applied for, then what?

The pastor becomes an encourager, an inspirer, an idea man, a promoter, a backstage prodder to see that the requirements outlined in the manual *A Road to Renewal* are carried out.

But if he wants a successful mission he must go further. He must play fair with his coordinators, his witnesses, and his people. If they are going to be praying for him then he must also be praying for them. If he is going to require a lot of advance reading on the part of his people then he, too, must be willing to read all the advance booklets and pamphlets usually associated with a mission.

If he is going to ask his people to come together in groups to pray for the mission he should attend some of these sessions as a fellow member of the group.

If the program calls for him to read several choice books in the field of prayer, the Holy Spirit, small groups, and church renewal he should do so.

The local pastor will have many courtesies to remember and carry out in regard to the visiting witnesses and the coordinator assigned his church.

The pastor might well remember that the coordinator is just as apprehensive about the local pastor as the pastor is about the coordinator. Therefore the pastor has a responsibility to make the coordinator feel wanted and at home. These two will often be together by themselves during the mission and there needs to be excellent rapport between them. Even though they may be tense from many duties they would do well to give the appearance of "hanging loose."

After the mission the pastor will work with his people to conserve the values of the mission. He will want to encourage the follow-up chairman as small groups are formed. His help will be needed to keep the groups alive and vital. He will suggest books to be read. His first sermons will be designed to help the people understand and expand on what has been happening to them. As a rule he will be running up against so many "coincidences" and so many thrilling encounters that he will find himself sharing his own newfound joys with others through the pulpit and in small groups.

His men will welcome him to a men's prayer group and he may want to join a couples' prayer group with his wife.

If experience continues to run true several of his people will be going on missions. He'll want to have a send-off prayer with them and to anticipate a report from them on their mission. There will be opportunities to counsel the over-eager ones to help them establish a healthy balance between staying home to serve and going on a mission.

Each pastor will react and respond according to his own nature, but inevitably he will be involved. It's a lay movement but there's a definite place for the pastor—a big and happy place.

Team Sessions

A considerable amount of time is involved by a host layman in a lay witness mission. He may or may not be aware that his visiting witnesses will be meeting even more than the local folk. Sandwiched in and around the local meetings are some four to six hours of team sessions. These are special, time-apart moments for the coordinator, the out of town witnesses, and a few of the local leaders of the mission. Present also is the local pastor who is keeping as quiet as the proverbial church mouse but who is happily basking in the warmth and fellowship of the team. Since he can't attend all the small group meetings he'll try to soak up as much of the spirit as possible at these sessions.

There are many words to describe the team sessions, especially the first one which is held at 5:30 on Friday soon after the arrival of the witnesses and prior to the first dinner meeting at 6:30 p.m. The descriptive words and phrases that come to mind are "contagious," "winsome," "exciting," "quick shedding of masks," "first name basis," "liquid love," "instant friendship," "vehicle of the Holy Spirit."

At the first session there is much anticipation as witnesses meet the host leaders, many of the other witnesses, and perhaps even their coordinator for the first time. For some these are moments of happy reunion as fellow witnesses from former missions meet again.

There is not much time to decide if you're scared, or if you like someone, or if the team is a good one. There is lots of praying to be done, because these people have learned to put the mission in the hands of God. Perhaps the local hosts will be introduced to conversational prayer for the first time. There are techniques for quickly getting on a first name basis, and for alleviating the anxieties of first timers. The coordinator, whether he is a "hang loose" person or a "master sergeant" type, is busy with orientation type comments; with being sure the witness is undergirded by prayer and Bible reading; with knowing his team by first names; with making the first night assignments of who will witness at the dinner table and who will lead the discussions.

The Saturday morning session is again full of laughter and a growing excitement. Everyone is a bit sleepy, considering the long ride on Friday, discussion and sharing sessions that for some ran rather late, plus the kitchen table snack and sharing sessions with their hosts for the weekend. But grogginess is soon sloughed off as the coffee assignments and luncheon assignments are made and as the prayer period is eagerly anticipated. Gone is the first uneasiness of the previous night and present is the fact they now know some people personally to lift in prayer. Needs are prayed for but confidences are kept. Reluctantly they break up at half past nine to meet their chauffeurs and head for the home where they are to lead or co-lead a valuable discussion period—hopefully a "let's drop our masks and get down to the real issues" sort of meeting.

The third team session comes about five-thirty following the full and eventful day. Prayer is still the chief order of the agenda but there are things to share and moments in which to evaluate the direction of the mission. Dinner assignments and discussion assignments follow.

The Sunday session, usually falling at 7:30 A.M. to allow for an early church service, really calls for an extra effort. Those discussion groups the night before just wouldn't stop—some going to midnight—then the people went in droves to the altar, some more tender moments with the host and hostess where you stay and all this adds up to a short night.

The session starts in a rather subdued fashion as weariness has its way. But soon the sharing of victories already won the night before begins to have its effect and weariness begins to be cast off. The final stretch is ahead. There is a church service, some church school classes to lead, and often a second service to anticipate.

It's the final stretch, the gun lap, and all systems are go. From somewhere comes the needed adrenalin and the team is born anew, unified, happy, and expectant.

This is the way the witnesses describe it:

"I have never known such love and joy as is displayed in the team sessions. The Holy Spirit is truly real and present. My whole being is so calmed and made receptive at these sessions. The last evidence of masks is removed and my real self comes out to love and share openly."

"I feel like the Holy Spirit is present in the team sessions and felt by everyone."

"I get the feeling of close fellowship, love, and the near presence of God and I don't feel alone."

"The mood I felt was a reverence and nearness to God. These team sessions helped me more than anything to prepare for the small group meetings. So the whole mission benefits from the team sessions."

"I was helped by the frankness among team members to express their own personal needs and weaknesses. I felt the Holy Spirit with us working through me and touching others in a way that is always a miracle."

These are some evaluations of the coordinators:

"From my experience, every session can be a vehicle for the work of the Holy Spirit. The team sessions offer periods in which the members of the team can strengthen one another in prayer as they ask the Holy Spirit to direct, strengthen, and open the hearts of all involved."

"From both the standpoint of the team member and from the standpoint of the coordinator, it is my impression that the team sessions are indispensable. It is here the team becomes a team in the unity of the spirit and a vessel which the Holy Spirit can use."

One believes that oral prayer—open conversation and supplication to God—is the key to our Protestant priesthood. As the team members share their concerns the team begins to interact, to lift one another in spirit and love, and finally becomes a Christ-centered team. Team sessions can be particularly used of the Holy Spirit in training and leading newer, less mature, more reluctant witnesses. "By such exercises as the Ros Rinker four step prayer sequence; standing in groups of three to love one another with no conversation, the oral definition of *who he is* to another in thirty seconds with no proper names or titles, the coordinator trains witnesses for closer, more effective, spirit-filled efforts. Team sessions cause one to look at something as Gert Behanna and say, 'Is this for the Lord, or is this for Gert?' "

Small Group Meetings

The word of the visiting witnesses and the local people is that the discussion groups on Friday night, Saturday morning, and Saturday night are the most productive during the lay witness mission.

On Friday night they have been put at ease and have begun to feel the reflected warmth of the visiting witnesses, and the secure feeling of the small secluded group. Among other devotional thoughts they will usually come face to face with two questions, "What do you want to see happen to your church this weekend?" and "What do you want to see happen in your own personal life?" You will talk and share and pray about these questions but in a very permissive attitude. No pressure will be exerted and timid or inhibited persons can "pass" their turn to speak.

When the groups meet for the coffees in the homes they have two things working for them. One, they are meeting in the relaxed atmosphere of a home, away from the church building, and two, they've had a night to think and speculate and even pray about what transpired the night before.

Hence when the coffee hour comes people are much more willing to relax and let their masks drop. As they become more open and honest with each other the more anxious they are for help and the more open they are to suggestions.

The close of the coffee hour comes before the participants are ready for adjournment. They have so much to ask or say that they want to linger on. So after a second cup of coffee the people will hang around informally for another productive hour, allowing just time to get to noon luncheons.

When the evening discussion hour arrives it has behind it all the witnessing, fellowship, discussions, and praying of the past twenty-four hours. In this period the people find a lot of cross-pollination from earlier groups and they meet new leaders from the visiting witnesses.

When these groups assemble after the supper hour and the witnessing, there are no hidebound closing times suggested because each group needs to be turned loose to develop at its own pace.

Fellowship Meals

As the movement grows and more experience is gained we

learn to put value on those things that contribute to the mood and spirit of the mission.

Many coordinators have found the mealtimes especially rewarding. For example, the Friday night mealtime is one of mounting excitement. Host congregations and visiting witnesses confront each other for the first time. The witnesses come freshly inspired from a team session and are scattered among the home people so they can get acquainted during the meal.

At the close of the meal the pastor introduces the coordinator who puts the people at ease. He introduces from two to four witnesses who seem to gain immediate rapport with the people.

In the informality at the table the host members begin to get the feel of the mission and to come under the spell of the visitors without the feeling of being hemmed in or put on the spot. Timid or inhibited persons can be somewhat loosened up by the experience of the dinner hour without feeling that all eyes are focused on them.

Large groups of people gathered informally for a common purpose generate enthusiasm. Since the Friday meal usually attracts the largest attendance the whole mission gets off to a good start on the weight of sheer numbers, be the people there out of dedication or out of simple curiosity.

The next two meals are the separate luncheons for men and women on Saturday. Experience has shown that mates often times are reluctant to open up in each other's presence. This will be true if prior to this time they had not been able to express intimate spiritual thoughts to each other. The separate luncheon affords an opportunity for men to react to men and women to women. Local people have come fresh from the coffees where people had begun to take off their masks. Menfolk are now ready for some manly companionship; for a chance to have a misty eye without destroying their image of the strong silent type who does not show emotion. Male witnesses from out of town can now share some more personal insights that have improved husband and wife relationships, or father and son relationships.

Likewise the women's luncheon is an occasion for 'women talk.' Witnesses gain immediate rapport when they confess to the same difficulties with children, or husband's work demands, or husband's lack of interest in the church. This has come to be known as leading from weakness. There can be much laughter also which has its own redeeming values. Family foibles and burdens are seen in a new light and endured and carried more graciously.

Sometimes near the end of the witnessing period the women are paired in twos for some heart to heart sharing. One woman listens intently as the other shares some deep "concern." When each has shared they often put their heads together to pray for each other.

The Saturday night meal becomes a joyous occasion for by now the witnesses are thoroughly accepted and friendships are developing. Table conversation carries a gayer and more relaxed mood. Witnesses not yet heard from will be on the program. Sometimes several are used at this point. It's a great time to get to know more witnesses and for local persons to get to know each other.

The Sunday luncheon furnishes a chance for newfound friends to say goodbye properly, and for hosts and house guests to see each other again.

A friendship circle with a lot of spontaneous singing and a closing prayer will long be remembered by one and all.

If the host people have this opportunity at the noon meal they are much more apt to return to the evaluation session later in the day. As will be pointed out elsewhere, "He who misses the evening sharing session is missing the climax of the whole mission."

Meals should be planned for in such a way as not to tie up a lot of personnel in the kitchen. You'll want all your Marthas to have a chance to hear the witnesses and participate in the discussion groups.

Sunday Schedule

Because so much of a minister's life is spent in building up to Sunday morning services he is acclimated to expect high moments in his ministry to happen at such services. He is not disappointed.

People come in large numbers to the services, sing with more enthusiasm, and smile with a greater radiance. There is an expectant feeling in the air. The service moves along on schedule and in good order.

The coordinator usually is the morning speaker as he witnesses for the first time. He speaks from the vantage point of several missions. His message is simple, sincere, and enthusiastic.

Although closing services vary from church to church experience has shown that many, many persons are deeply moved at this time. And of those who are moved many of them will quietly and quickly come to kneel at the altar or in rows behind those at the altar. A period of prayer follows, a benediction is pronounced, and the service is over.

People have gone to the altar who haven't been in church for months or even years; people are there who haven't been to an altar since they were married. In fact husbands and wives are often there with hands clasped—reaffirming a solid relationship or pledging themselves to a fresh start, a renewed effort to recapture something of the old magic. New possibilities have been opened up and commitments to these possibilities have been made. And a joyous spirit that goes with new resolutions prevails. Life is suddenly made better, everyone around seems like a friend. The milling about, the tarrying in the aisles, in the foyers, and on the sidewalks goes on and on.

The witnesses are the centers of little clusters of people. It's all a postlude to meaningful moments and a prelude for even more to come.

And that wondering preacher begins to believe that the time to wonder is over. Maybe the final assurance won't come until that night, but enough of the evidence is in to send the preacher off to the farewell luncheon with a new spirit of optimism.

The Evaluation

To use a frivolous comparison the evaluation session is the cherry on top of the dessert. The whole weekend with its delights and thrills has been building up to Sunday night. When it gets there the home folks are on their own. The team of persons who came to share are now gone.

The home folks come with wonder and anticipation in their hearts. After a song or two the chairman asks if anyone has anything to say. Someone breaks the ice and the meeting is underway. By description from scores of persons it often become the "greatest meeting ever held in our church."

It is here that the pastor feels closer than ever to his people, where he is accepted as a person, where he sees a a newer side of his parishioners.

Hints to Host Churches

1. Because potentially a lot of good interaction can take place between visiting witnesses and local hosts, the local housing committee should take care when they assign the witnesses. Sometimes a committee reasons that if they will put a witness with an inactive family maybe they can reclaim that particular family. What so often happens in these cases is that the host family does not participate. This robs the witness of a time to share with his hosts, and makes for a bit of embarrassment also.

2. Another hint is in terms of the meals at the church. Try to plan them in such a way as not to tie up a lot of persons in the kitchen. You want all the local people possible free to attend the sessions. Also it is recommended that the meals be open to the general congregation on Friday night, Saturday night, and Sunday noon. There are positive values to be gained by doing so.

3. When you write your witnesses to invite them to come, type or write each letter personally. This is a small matter but an appreciated one. Make each invitation a personal one. This will help to convey the idea that you care.

In the matter of letters be sure to write the letters of

invitation as soon as you get your list from the coordinator. If a witness tells a coordinator he'll go if invited and the letter doesn't come for weeks he begins to wonder if he is going to be invited, and if the local people are truly getting ready for the mission. Your delay in writing might prevent the witness from accepting other invitations while waiting to hear from you.

4. After a mission is over get your thank you notes off soon. The witnesses are very anxious to hear what took place Sunday night and what the follow through seems to be.

It would help immeasurably if you would tape record and transcribe the remarks made at the evaluation session. If that is not possible have a recorder who will attempt to take down the statements made. Send copies of these as soon as possible to all your guest witnesses.

5. Do everything in your power to involve many people in prayer and preparation for the mission. A twenty-four hour prayer vigil would involve a lot of people and greatly enhance the spirit of the mission.

6. Follow the lay witness mission manual very carefully. Do not cut corners. Make full preparation in every area called for in the manual. As the mission gets underway you see the fruits of your efforts and understand more fully the reasons for full preparation.

7. In addition to the preparation called for in the manual try to determine from the coordinator the things he would like to see carried out. As a witness and as a coordinator he will have observed things which will enhance your mission.

8. When the mission is over you will have a group who has gone through a thrilling experience, and another group who missed out on the experience. It is very important not to let wedges come between the two groups. The newfound happiness of the one group is hard to contain. This group will need to be reminded that there is more than one way to come into a personal relationship with Christ—that a man can be a man of deep faith and not have been through a mission. Let none of your actions imply that these people are lacking in true

faith. Share and have fellowship with them but do not imply a superiority of experience.

The Follow Through

The work of a lay witness mission does not stop with the departure of the witnesses nor with the last testimony at the evaluation session. The real lasting work is just beginning. The work of conserving present gains, of adding to those gains, and of deeper involvement in the "mission of the church" is yet to come.

The follow-up chairman has an important task to carry out. This chairman is to help in the formation of prayer groups, sharing groups, Bible study groups, and special discipline groups.

There will be plenty of help at this point. Many groups will spring up almost automatically. Couples or individuals who have had an enriching experience will gather about them a group of other interested persons, choose a night and place to meet and they are off and running.

The follow-up chairman will do a lot of coordinating as he discovers the groups and the nights and seeks to assimilate others into these groups. He will also be concerned in keeping a live spirit going among the groups and with seeing that they have plenty of guidance resources and study materials.

For a while the groups will be content to share and pray but with time they'll ask for something to sink their teeth into.

These groups will develop in many divergent ways according to the personalities of the members of the groups.

For those who want to know more about the many possible discipline groups, the book, *Koinonia Ministries Guidebook,* by Walter Albritton is highly recommended, along with the six Focus handbook series. All are available from Tidings.

As the small groups progress they will find themselves needing to be on guard against the pitfalls that any small group in the church has to watch for.

Here are a few suggestions:

1. If people are to gain maximum help they must have a

group they can trust before they can be fully honest—so each person must carefully remember not to disclose confidences shared in such a group.

2. It would be best where feasible to rotate the weekly sessions from house to house, carefully avoiding trying to outdo the others on refreshments. In fact it is suggested that you by-pass refreshments.

3. If prayer is your chief purpose for gathering then get right down to the business of praying. Save your small talk until later, or else you'll small-talk your time away.

4. It is also a point of wisdom to rotate the leadership of the group each week, thus helping more persons to grow, and thus avoiding the group being built around a person instead of Jesus Christ.

5. Watch the meeting time, or else you may stay too long and cause a shortage of sleep in too many families.

6. To keep your group a redemptive fellowship do not allow critical words to be spoken of persons. A group that becomes a gossip session very quickly loses its power.

7. As you grow in these groups do not expect everyone else to keep pace with you. Different groups and different individuals will be working at their own pace. At this point it might be well to caution against expecting your preacher to keep abreast of you in all your specialized reading and your deepening spiritual understanding. Ministers have a total congregation to which they must minister. They cannot limit themselves to that small percentage of their people who come under the influence of the lay witness mission. So if he suddenly doesn't seem "spiritual" enough as a result of your having gone through a mission, don't criticize him. Understand his total task and pray for him.

"And day by day, attending the temple together and breaking bread in their homes, they partook of food with glad and generous hearts, praising God and having favor with all the people." (Acts 2:46-47*a*)

6

Facing Honest Questions About Results

Many questions are being asked by interested persons. To get some answers we asked these questions of the host pastors involved in our study.

1. Now that the mission is over how do you see the concept of the ministry of the laity? How do you plan to involve laymen in a ministry to the congregation, to the community, and to the world?

"At the present time I have not had to involve my laymen in ministry to the congregation, to the community, or the world—they have involved themselves in some ways I never dreamed possible."

"We have more young married men taking part than in the past. We have laymen leading renewal groups, a number going on lay witness missions, and one has been made a coordinator."

"My laymen are visiting prospects and absentees, and witnessing to the local congregation."

"We have a number of people who do carry a concern for the mission of the world. This concern was strengthened and we are seeking ways of involvement."

"The concept of 'the ministry of the laity' becomes more realistic."

"My people are more interested in visiting than ever before. We are studying *New Forms of Missions* in joint sessions of our prayer groups."

"Our church supports and staffs a day kindergarten in an underprivileged area, a rescue mission for derelicts, and a bridgehouse for alcoholics. It sponsors two kindergarten classes for children of the community; it has increased its voluntary help to several local hospitals; it has bought a three acre lot in the mountains for a new church; and helps with a mobile ministry to Indians on the reservation. These projects did not grow out of the mission but participation in them has been greatly increased by the inspiration of the mission."

"There is involvement in the local church, in organizing groups, in visitation, and in worship services."

2. What forms of witnessing other than talking can you see coming out of your experiences with a mission?

"One of the greatest forms of witnessing to come out of this has been people praying with one another."

"We have some who express their love for others in thoughtful deeds, and in praying and sharing."

"They are witnessing with their lives, a radiant thing in itself. Some are speaking of witnessing with their tithe and service."

"They witness by joining a prayer group and by starting their own prayer life. From this comes a concern to work with and understand others."

"The most effective form of witnessing is not in talking, but in living the life of Christian love. I see this in the actions and concerns of those touched by the mission for others."

3. Are your people who were affected favorably by the mission still doing the workhouse chores, the nitty-gritty duties someone has to do?

"The same reliable ones are."

"Yes."

"We have some new workers in our groups, but most are the regular faithful members who carry on their chores."

"Yes, but with a new spirit."

"Yes, a goodly number are still willing to carry on."

"There is a new willingness to volunteer to do the routine and sometimes unglamorous chores that have to be done to keep our organization functioning."

Other Outside Questions

1. Is it wise to offer people a big enthusiastic weekend that some term an emotional jag?

Assuming for a moment that it was only a weekend jag, would there be anything awful about that? Don't we go to a basketball tournament involving our team and have a big emotional time? Does it destroy our love for a basketball game between our team and our traditional rival? Does this big emotion-ridden spree cure us of basketball fever? Then why not afford the same privilege to the lay witness mission?

But let us hasten on to say that the lay witness mission is not a one-shot emotional experience. It eventuates in small groups that enhance and keep alive the spiritual values gained from the mission. The praying, the studying, the devotional use of the Bible all work together to conserve what was started by the mission.

Granted that we cannot stay on the mountain forever we can still use mountaintop experiences to deepen our faith. As one university counselor reports: "Every time I come off the mountaintop I stop further up the slope from the valley than the time before."

If the emotional experience of a mission brings about a deepening of faith and launches people on a daily schedule of prayer, Bible study, and service then it is a wise procedure.

2. Are lay witnesses seeking to avoid involvement in the social issues of the day by going on missions?

We see no real evidence that this is true. True enough there is a certain amount of excitement about going on missions at first, in their zealousness to share, the feeling is that they want to go every weekend. But this soon balances itself out—what with money problems and the problems of small children. They go, say, once a month, get their batteries recharged and then cheerfully carry on at home the other three weeks.

3. Have church programs been seriously curtailed because witnesses are spending money on missions that formerly went to such programs?

Thus far we have not heard of any place that this has

happened. Paradise Hills in Albuquerque has several active witnesses and yet their financial picture has greatly improved since their mission. Other churches have reported several new tithers among their witnesses.

4. Are local church programs seriously affected by the occasional absence of a witness from his church?

Not seriously so. Sometimes several leaders might be absent on a key Sunday. Sometimes a substitute teacher or usher has to take over, but these are offset by the advantages. The absentees come back renewed and refreshed and willing to work with a new spirit. Their stories of changed lives inspire us all and we all get a reflected renewal from hearing from each witness.

"Who then is the faithful and wise servant, whom his master has set over his household, to give them their food at the proper time? Blessed is that servant whom his master when he comes will find so doing." (Matthew 24:45-46)

7

Probing the Nature of a Mission

Psychological Principles at Work

With no desire at this point to launch into a learned discussion on the psychology of religion let us point out that psychological principles can be observed in the various activities of a lay witness mission.

In a prayer group one morning, where there were some electrical engineers present, we talked a bit about electrical concepts that could be applied to what we had seen and heard in missions and in follow-up groups.

One term was *induction.* Human engineers have borrowed this term from the electrical men. It simply is the principle whereby one coil placed within the field of another becomes charged, although it is not in direct contact with the electrical source. This is seen to be functioning in the missions. Local persons are often charged and moved at first toward an experience of their own when they see and hear the exuberant or serene witnesses on Friday night and in the subsequent group sessions. A non-church-going host visits with his guest and comes under the spell of his winsomeness and declares, "I want what that young man has." Appetites are whetted through the process of induction.

There is another electrical term that has some bearing in the total experience of a mission. It is called *polarity.* It's a term used to show how individuals are drawn to a person, or an ideal, or a common objective that will unify them. It is this process that will produce a *homogeneity* of purpose and interest. This calls for a center around which to rally. It intensifies emotion in people, it causes them to reinforce each other, and to build up enthusiasm. Apply these statements to what you see taking place in the course of a mission. Do we not see rallying ideas, emotion, reinforcement, and enthusiasm at every turn?

In talking about principles we should not overlook *inter-stimulation.* This is to say that the presence of others in a group influences each of the persons present. The recorded testimony of the witnesses often reflects this principle at work in the team sessions, the group discussions, the larger dinner groups and the church services. We tend to alter our conduct, to have our interest stimulated, and our activity intensified because of the presence of others. We find ourselves being influenced intellectually and emotionally because of others. The presence of others on a similar search for religious insight will heighten the emotional tone of a group. One of the happy delights of a mission is the inter-stimulation that takes place.

Another principle which has a bit of a chance to work at a mission is *interaction.* Here people meet or work in twos, fours, eights, tens, and so forth to exchange views, to give suggestions, even to sometimes disagree. It's all a part of being civilized or of being a democracy. It's a good balancing agent. Without a tag being put on it this principle gets in its licks during the group activities of a mission.

Another principle not to be overlooked in such an activity is *mutual indentification.* Sometimes it seems as if this principle goes to work more quickly in a mission than in other situations. It is our ability to feel with others even though not afflicted ourselves. It's sometimes called understanding or empathy. Some people call it the most potent and most nearly universal socializing influence in society. It must be potent because it is amazing how quickly rapport, and understanding, and sympathy, and empathy are established in a mission between visiting witnesses and host lay people. Of course there are many degrees of this depending on many factors. But time and time again we get cases of "instant friendship" or "instant love" after a few short hours of contact in a mission.

From the area of group dynamics we get new ways of looking at ourselves in relation to others and to the world. Here we deal with a man's life thesis, the nature of the interaction taking place, the strategies that seem appropriate to the life thesis, and to the kind of interaction that would be most fruitful.

Every person must eventually ask himself the questions: "What kind of a person am I to become? Am I going to be an exploiter of other persons in my relationship to them? Am I going to be an isolated individual distrustful of any close personal relationship? Am I to be a cooperator with other persons?" This last question leads us to hazard the statement if we are to have much significance in the world we will want to become a part of a cluster of persons having the same desire to make their lives significant.

Certainly these insights of group dynamics are to be found at work in lay witness missions. Cooperation goes into the preparation of a mission and certainly into the execution of one.

We have no documented cases of exploiters or distrustful people making sudden turnabouts, but we have observed many a harsh edge taken off the personality of a mission participant.

Now lay witness mission witnesses, no matter what their degree of competence might be, do not go to host churches to be psychologists or psychiatrists. In fact they are strongly advised not to do so. A fine religious experience on their part does not create an "instant" psychoanalyst or therapist.

Even so, some mild, and perhaps at times not so mild, therapy does take place as a result of the varying kinds of group action to be found in the framework of a mission. This comes in part as a by-product of the elements present in most, if not all, sessions.

Therapy succeeds where there is unconditional love, where there is a permissive environment, and where a person's growth and development are conditioned by the group's values and attitudes.

Now, keeping these principles or conditions in mind as you recall the group experiences of missions you have known, would you not say that these were present in varying degrees? Granted that here and there an individual group session might flunk out or come to a stalemate or an impasse, the larger experience of missions has been that these principles are actively at work bringing about growth experiences of great value.

No clinical effort is made to ask a person to question himself, but a person could if necessary examine himself in this fashion after a mission. Do I see myself as more integrated? Am I able to be more spontaneous and genuine? Am I capable of better coping with the problems life puts before me? Can I look at myself more objectively? Can I be objective toward my abilities and characteristics with greater personal comfort?

If a person has positive responses to make to these questions then, without consciously setting out to do so, he has benefited from the elements of group therapy found to be inherent in a mission.

To borrow further from the field of group processes let us summarize some over-all criteria:

1. Was it a permissive group?
2. Was it an understanding group where you viewed your problems from the perspective of others having the same problems?
3. Was it a group dedicated to the highest possible fulfillment of each other?
4. Was it a group that experienced a crisis together and had the strength to meet it?
5. Was it a group which accepted the individual member in the role they had envisioned for themselves?
6. Was it a group willing to take time to allow the members to grow?
7. Was it a group whose first concern was to become a group and after that a concern to look at the action undertaken?
8. Could hungry people talk about the serious things of life?

9. Could people get emotional release by saying what they honestly thought and felt without being exiled from the group's favor?

10. Did the group encourage rather than stifle creative thought?

11. Did the group have enough time together to really become a group?

We would want to again state that these are not often conscious considerations on the part of witnesses or host participants, before, during, or after a lay witness mission. However, should such a person be asked to examine his mission experience in the light of these questions our contention is that the questions would in the majority of cases receive a resounding positive answer.

This writer realizes that such a cold impartial look at our experiences may arouse the displeasure of those who want to preserve the spontaneity of the mission movement, where the Holy Spirit is not programmed or structured, and where a witness's sincerity is not inhibited by a pat set of instructions.

To such persons who might be offended we apologize and ask you to take comfort in the other chapters where we seek to report with more subjective warmth.

Theological Content

There is not room in a report such as this for an exhaustive treatise on all the theological implications of the lay witness movement. Two beliefs considered to be uniquely associated with Methodism, however, will be considered.

First, there is the doctrine of Christian experience. We have long declared that "every person can experience God through Jesus Christ; that assurance and peace come to those who have the experience; that whereas this experience often comes in a single moment called conversion, it is repeated again and again as one has fellowship with Christ and surrenders his life to Him." (Refer to Spiritual Life Chart, published by Tidings.)

The witness of scores of persons who have participated in missions is that they do, time and time again, come to an experience of God through a confrontation with Jesus Christ. Methodists stress experience and certainly thousands have a new peace and a new assurance they have never known before. This sometimes comes as a direct result of participation in a mission or as a result of participation in the follow up groups.

Those who carry through on the follow-up—quiet time, Bible reading, sharing, praying—witness that their commitment or dedication is not a one time affair but a series of fresh dedications. With each new dedication comes a sense of peace and assurance.

The second meaningful doctrine that is related to lay missions is known as the witness of the spirit. This thought permeates much of the teaching of the Bible and is perhaps best described by Paul as he wrote to the folks at Rome, "The Spirit itself beareth witness with our spirit, that we are children of God: And if children, then heirs; heirs of God, and joint-heirs with Christ; if so be that we . . . may be also glorified together." (Romans 8:16-17)

This is by way of saying that God has a way of making his presence known in our hearts—the Holy Spirit giving his own proof of his presence through experience.

John Wesley, learned scholar that he was, admitted that it was hard to find words in the language of men to explain the deep things of God. He went on to say though that by an inward impression of the soul "the Spirit of God immediately and directly witnesses to my spirit, that I am a child of God; that Jesus Christ hath loved me, and given Himself for me; that all my sins are blotted out, and I, even I, am reconciled to God."

Wesley looked at that statement twenty years after making it and said he did not need to retract any of it nor seek to improve upon it.

He went on to say that he did not mean that the Spirit spoke with an outward voice or always with an inward voice, or always through a pointed Scripture, but the Spirit so "works upon the Soul by His immediate influence . . . that the stormy wind and troubled waves subsided, and there is sweet calm. . . ."

Wesley was a troubled and anxious person for many years of his early ministry. After his famous heartwarming experience at Aldersgate he experienced greater peace of mind and an assurace not previously felt. Because of his own personal experience Wesley's thought perceived God's Spirit as entering human life and bearing witness to its presence.

As Wesley talked about the doctrine of assurance critics labeled it enthusiasm. Wesley felt the doctrine to be too important to give up just because it could be distorted. So he protected it by insisting that those who claim the assurance of the working of the Spirit in their lives must at the same time show the fruits of the Spirit.

As one reads or hears constant testimony that the Holy Spirit was felt over and over again in lay missions, and as one observes the persons making the testimony it is obvious that many pass Wesley's test. It goes beyond the realm of sheer enthusiasm when the fruits become so obvious. Love, joy, and peace abound in a mission and its follow up groups. Observe the lives of those truly caught up in the spirit of a mission and see the changes wrought. See a meekness, a gentleness, an ability for long-suffering not previously manifested.

Not many persons can verbalize just how this takes place. I cannot say. But one thing they can say is that it did take place. They know because they have experienced it.

Someone in writing about Pentecost pointed out the conditions that made possible the coming of the Holy Spirit into the early church. There was *expectancy*, there was *unity*, there was *constancy* and *persistency*, there was *receptivity*, and there was *consecrated activity*. Using these phrases you could write a book about lay witness missions.

After months of preparation there is a great sense of expectancy in the air as the mission approaches and particularly as Friday night arrives. For months there has been a unity building up among the committeemen and the visiting team quickly becomes a unit. For weeks some people have constantly and persistently believed that something great was going to happen, that the Holy Spirit would be known amongst the people.

And certainly there is an eager receptivity. The soil is ready, hearts are open to the Holy Spirit. Just as there was consecrated activity at Pentecost so there is at lay witness missions. These people believe that they must share what they have found with others, that if they attempt to keep it they will lose it. Give it out or give it up. The early churchmen knew they could not keep the Good News, except as they told it to others. And so it is still today. After each mission there are persons who will joyfully become witnesses to go to other churches to share their newfound joy.

As indicated earlier there are other theological considerations besides the doctrines of experience and of the witness of the spirit that apply to lay witness missions. We mention these two in brief because these are two with which the hosts and the guests can quickly identify and relate.

Those desiring to explore the matter further would do well to read a Tidings book *A Theology for Christian Witnessing* by Harvey Potthoff.

"Go therefore and make disciples of all nations, baptizing them in the name of the Father and of the Son and of the Holy Spirit, teaching them to observe all that I have commanded you." (Matthew 28: 19-20*a*)

8

Positive Values for the Church

There are many positive values that emanate from lay witness missions. As these values are put to work in the main stream of the church then the church gains a relevancy and a virility sadly lacking in some churches.

For instance, many gain a disciplined way of life, a closer attention to the holy habits, a better use of time. These gains will be reflected in the health of the church. Modern Protestants have been accused of having spiritual malnutrition. The lay witness mission seems to have the needed prescription at this point.

As much as any movement currently working in the life of the church lay witness missions are causing people to read and study the Bible. They are reading many versions of the Scriptures, especially *Good News for Modern Man.* They read not only for inspiration but for marching orders.

Through a mission and the follow-up groups people learn more about praying than in any other short period of time. Conversational prayer comes naturally with them and they seem to communicate with God with greater ease.

A lay witness mission awakens appetities for deeper spiritual growth. A hunger for reality seems to be apparent and people will join in a common search for reality. The missions are vehicles for initiating personal renewal. Any movement that initiates and enhances a search for reality and a deeper spiritual growth is bound to be helpful.

Lay witness missions have a way of relaxing inhibitions about witnessing. People who have been too timid, too frightened, or held back by feelings of inadequacy, or who felt it was taboo, are able, as a result of a mission experience, to witness for Christ wherever they may be. The church is blessed indeed when it has a goodly number of people who are not ashamed to say a good word for Jesus Christ.

Another positive value for the life of the church is that people will continue to do the needed tasks in the church but now they will do them for the right reasons. Whereas many acted from duty or out of loyalty to the pastor now they carry out their tasks with love and joy. Doing things for the right reasons will cause them to be healthier persons religiously speaking, and their work will be more productive of desired results.

As a result of local people being able to open up and level with each other honestly therapy has a chance to work. This makes for healthier people from an emotional viewpoint. As barriers between factions are eliminated the church gains in strength and unity.

A heightened sense of teamwork between the laymen and their pastors is a valuable outcome of a mission. Each sees and appreciates the other's role and the team begins to pull in harness together.

A corollary to this is the fact that laymen come to see their pastor and pastor's wife as human beings subject to human foibles like anyone else. Laymen are more willing to accept the pastor and his wife at face value and to love and respect them for what they are.

A minister's wife comes out of a mission with a sense of being accepted as a person in her own right. As a result solid friendships become possible between the minister's wife and women in the church. This new relationship can be most meaningful to one who never knows whether she is a minister's wife or a layman. These new friendships are also a blessing to the ministers' wives long classified as the "loneliest individuals in the world."

One of the goals of the established church is to change lives. Evidence from many missions is that lives are constantly being changed. If the changing process can be accelerated through the work of a mission then missions are adding much to the on-going life of the church. One veteran pastor and author in the field of evangelism has declared that he saw more lives changed in three days than he had seen in a year of his preaching. He was not planning on giving up preaching but was simply acknowledging what he had seen and felt.

An experienced witness and coordinator brings up a point that would seem to have a great bearing on the life of the church. In his travels and contacts he has met many churchmen who have a great insecurity as far as salvation is concerned, and also as far as their daily walk in life is concerned. He feels that not only is this a frustrating plight, it also inhibits their finding any real growth through Christ's church. "We are told Biblically," he says, "that God makes two free offers to us all. One offer is eternal life through our acceptance of Christ, and he tells us that this sets us free from the penalty of our sins. Then he offers to set us free from the power of our sin through the strength that is available through the Holy Spirit. One of the greatest accomplishments of a lay witness mission is getting across these points by means of the witnesses who are just everyday people sharing through their experiences how the reality of salvation and the work of the Spirit has changed their lives."

A dedicated and perceptive witness and coordinator expounds on a theme that is being touched upon by other writers in the field of church renewal. "I am convinced that the next great revival in our time will come through the efforts of the laity. We simply outnumber the ministers and thus it only makes good sense that our thrust can be so much stronger if we can all get headed in the right direction."

He puts out a challenge that ministers should do well to meditate upon. He believes that the revival will call upon the ordained clergy to accept a new place and a new role. "Your role," he says, "should now become that of coach, advisor, teacher. No longer should you have to be the leader. You will now have to be in a position to assist us as we become awakened laymen. You will have to teach us how to pray, how to study, how to witness, how to serve . . . all the things you have been wanting to teach your people for all these years, should now become part of your daily concern. I know that many ministers are afraid of our awakened laity because they feel they will lose out somehow. I see it as just the opposite. I see you fellows having the times of your lives getting to direct people in their search for a higher plane of life."

Now quite apart from the preceding discussion the lay witness mission is bringing new life and zest to many ministers. Young men who have become disillusioned with the church, disturbed by the status quo, and confused by their own seeming ineffectiveness have received a new lease on their ministerial life. Some of the dreams and hopes of beginning seminary days and something of the gleam and glint of ordination services comes back into their ministry.

Middle-aged ministers who have been caught up in a web of sermons to preach and a lot of hospital calls to make, and long committee meetings to sit through, all with little evidence of lives being changed or people becoming very excited about religion—these men are being renewed. They have a new hope they had despaired of having. They have the encouragement needed not only "to keep on keeping on" but to forge ahead once more. Instead of wistfully and longingly looking forward to retirement they begin to look forward to many more years of service.

Who can estimate the ultimate consequences to the life of the church through a battery of renewed and rededicated ministers? We speak here not only of the men who are renewed through seeing what happened to their laymen, but of the men who also experienced renewed and changed hearts.

"And every one who hears these words of mine and does not do them will be like a foolish man who built his house upon the sand; and the rain fell, and the floods came, and the winds blew and beat against that house, and it fell; and great was the fall of it." (Matthew 7:26-27)

Epilogue

This is being written several months after the original manuscript and a year after the Christ Church mission. I have now moved to a new community, have hosted another fine mission, have helped with other missions, have seen my high school daughter and wife off on several missions, have seen my son and a college age daughter deeply moved by missions, and have developed a host of friends through the missions.

In addition, I have watched the continued personal growth of many of the people caught up in the Christ Church mission. Four men are coordinating regularly and others would if their jobs permitted. Many go regularly on missions. As far as can be determined, most of them still work hard in their local church between mission trips.

At the point of witnesses being gone from their local churches, I like the comment of a nearby pastor who wrote, "After fifteen years in the ministry, I am having a new experience. I'm used to having people absent for sports, for hunting, for trips; now when I see holes left in the congregation I know they are absent because they are carrying the message of God's love to other communities. What a heartwarming feeling this brings to a pastor."

In retrospect, let me affirm that I strongly believe that the values to be gained from lay witness missions far outweigh the disadvantages. It is a movement of the Spirit whose time has come and we would do well to join forces with it.

In themselves, the missions are good. As a stepping stone to continued growth and development they are even better.

I want to go so far as to say that in all my long ministry I have never experienced a movement with the power and promise of these missions. If our ministers would throw themselves behind these efforts and would work hard to prepare their own hearts for a new infusion of the Spirit we could have the long-prayed-for renewal of the ministry and the laity. What a team for the kingdom we would then be.

To the pastor, local church, or individual layman, who is currently on the fence, let me respectfully suggest that you honestly try a mission, giving it your full support—and then accept what you can and let the rest pass by. In the meantime, you, your church, and your people will be stronger for the effort.

Postlude

"There was a man who went out to sow. As he scattered the seed in the field, some of it fell along the path, and the birds came and ate it up. Some of it fell on rocky ground, where there was little soil. The seeds soon sprouted, because the soil wasn't deep. When the sun came up it burned the young plants, and because the roots had not grown deep enough the plants soon dried up. Some of the seed fell among thorns, which grew up and choked the plants. But some seeds fell in good soil, and bore grain: some had one hundred grains, others sixty, and others thirty. And Jesus said, 'Listen, then, if you have ears!' " (Matthew 13:3-9)